LOVING IT ALL

Living with an Awakening Heart

DAVID BANNER PHD

ISBN: 1494788314
ISBN 13: 9781494788315

ADVANCE PRAISE FOR
LOVING IT ALL

Endorsements

"David delivers a guide on how to love ourselves and use that power to live a vibrant life. With the Enneagram as a tool, David shows you a simple approach to discovering a personal road map to live beyond self-imposed limitations. If you are ready to be bold and own your life, this is the book for you."
-Thomas White, CEO, C-Suite Network, Inc.

"Here's a safe prediction: David's latest book, Loving It All, will become a life-changing experience for a significant number of his readers. It's vividly different. For one thing, it is eminently readable, with Dave's warm, open heart shining through. For another, it is practical. He presents well-known concepts like "What your resist, persists", in a profoundly innovative way. Bottom line? The book is a powerful catalyst. Strap in and dive deep into the next chapter in your personal growth adventure."
-Will Wilkinson, co-author of Forgiving the Unforgivable, Awakening from the American Dream

David Banner's insights are timeless and universal, but particularly geared for—and needed in—these days of perilous climate change and economic fragility. Our actions on behalf of the planet can be far more effective if undertaken from stance of inner peace and deep connectedness with all life—in a word, love.
--Richard Heinberg
Author of Memories & Visions of Paradise, The Party's Over, and The End of Growth

David Banner offers an excellent handbook for the important work of bringing awareness the habitual ego distortions that so often live out as ego patterns in our life. His emphasis on love and acceptance of what is,

learning to relax resistance - a time-tested practice that will be a helpful companion on the journey of anyone sincere in their desire to awaken.
Miranda Macpherson, founder of 'Awakening Love & Wisdom' foundation, Author of 'Boundless love'.
www.mirandamacpherson.com

David Banner is one of the wisest men we know. We've devoured his other books, featured him as a Vision-Holder in our programs and consider him to be among the 10 visionaries we follow for what is emerging now in the culture. His new book, Loving it All, is a coherent, comprehensive and brilliant call to consciousness from a man who is passionate about a world that works for all.
Craig & Patricia Neal
Co-Authors of The Art of Convening

David writes with brilliance and passion. In Loving It All, he bestows upon us the gift of this brilliance with great clarity. You may not concur with all he presents, but he provides both depth and light. You will benefit from his wisdom and vast knowledge and underlying care. As he points out we all have a shadow side that needs to be owned, faced, and released. This is a must read. Thank you David.
David Daniels, M.D. clinical professor of psychiatry, Stanford Medical School and co-founder of Enneagram Studies in the Narrative Tradition
Co-author, THE ESSENTIAL ENNEAGRAM

In a bold new book, Loving it All, David Banner has devised a constructive roadmap to unconditional love and acceptance in a world fraught with war, injustice and fear. His concepts unveil the root causes of our

negativity and offer up a means of discovering love and acceptance,
allowing us to view the world in a more spiritual, open-minded way.
Sandy Garfunkel
Writer/Director, "Perhaps Tomorrow" - "Out of the Ash"
web: www.outoftheashmovie.com

ACKNOWLEDGEMENTS

I have been blessed with many teachers on my path towards awakening.

First of all, I would like to mention Ram Dass, whose seminal book, BE HERE NOW (1970) , opened me up to Eastern thought and to something real beyond the dogma of my church upbringing.

My dear friend and spiritual mentor, Thomas White, whose profound wisdom and gracious love for me is always a gift.

My mentors on the written page, e.g., Deepak Chopra, Eckhart Tolle. Byron Katie, Adyashanti, Charles Eisenstein and Jeff Fisher, to name a few; these folks have encouraged me through their words to explore my true identity.

My wonderful mentors in the Emissaries of Divine Light, Uranda, Lord Martin Cecil, and Alan Hammond, who taught me about the practicality of spiritual living.

My wife of 30 years, Diane, whose radiance, grace, innocence and love for service have inspired me greatly.

And my outstanding editor, Ms. Loma Huh, who famously kept saying "this makes no sense" or "where did you get that assertion?"; she kicked my rear end with such loving kindness.

Any errors of omission or commission are mine alone.

David K. Banner, PhD
Viroqua, WI
February, 2014

.

TABLE OF CONTENTS

CHAPTER 1

CHAPTER 2

CHAPTER 3

Healing the Shadow   29

CHAPTER 4

The Role of Gratitude   39

CHAPTER 5

The Role of Service   51

CHAPTER 6

The Present Moment   59

CHAPTER 7

A Return to Oneness   67

CHAPTER 8

The Awakened Heart   75

CHAPTER 9

CHAPTER 10

Introduction

A crucial awakening is occurring right now in the human race: an awakening from the sleepwalking state of duality, where7 the human ego is in charge and wreaking havoc all around, into the reality of oneness and of *non-dual* identity and function. What does this mean? It means a movement toward our true function as conscious beings who were meant to tend and keep the garden of our earthly paradise.

All our worldly systems created by sleepwalking humans are crumbling under their own density. By propagating the illusion of duality, mankind has created wars, pollution, and notions of good and bad that contribute to the unsustainable state of separateness. In this book, I seek to illustrate how we got into this situation and how we might extract ourselves from it.

Before I go any further, I want to state my assumptions, which will help you understand my perspective. You may not agree with them, and that is fine. But to understand the book, you need to know these assumptions:

1. We chose each incarnation on Earth and, in choosing, we choose our parents, our location, our life circumstance…all of it. We chose this to have certain experiences for our evolutionary growth. So a child born into a dustbowl in Ethiopia, the people killed by the militant Muslims in the Mumbai hotel massacre, folks killed by drone strikes all chose, at the soul level, to have those experiences.

2. The first assumption *does not* mean that they chose this consciously.

3. There are no victims, persecutors or rescuers in reality. We all are 100 percent responsible for our experiences. However, saying

that you are 100 percent responsible *does not* mean you are to blame at all (see, for example, Michael Durst, *Napkin Notes on the Art of Living*, 1990).

4. Everything that shows up in our experience *must* be contained within us as potential for it to show up at all (for more on this, see Ho'oponopono, the Hawaiian spiritual process for clearing out old wounds in your consciousness).

5. The Divine Design, the current of Life flowing through you, the God-force within you (all say the same thing) has a design for your life. If you follow this design, you will experience joy and fulfillment. If you choose not to follow it and instead allow the egoic, fear-based mind to dictate your choices, you will experience suffering. Anything that is out of alignment with the creative force of the Universe will produce ill effects.

6. You have complete free will at all times. If you choose to follow the dictates of Spirit for your life, you will reach your potential and be a blessing in your world; if you allow the egoic mind to rule, ups and downs will prevail. *And*, in following Spirit, this might even mean you die a so-called premature death, if that's in the design for your life.

7. What you see "out there" is never reality; rather, it is a mind-made fiction composed of a projection from your belief systems, attitudes, values and expectations, overlaid on whatever the genuine reality is.

8. Your incarnation is a precious thing; don't waste it!

My premise is this: If we create our reality with our thoughts, beliefs and attitudes, if we are living in our own "mind-made" world, the path to healing requires that we take responsibility for our creation by welcoming everything that comes to us—the things we like and the things we don't like. When we accept what is without resistance, we create space for it to change; when we resist it, our pushing against it locks it into place.

This, of course, runs counter to what we have been taught to believe. We have been taught to judge things as good or bad, and then accept what we like and reject what we don't like. An example of this might be when we don't like our weight; so, feeling depressed, we resist our weight and we eat even more! And this is what the human ego does; it is a false identity that judges good and bad, right/wrong, black/white, and decides how things should be.

This resistance to what *is* causes a lot of the suffering in the world. What is, is exactly what is; no amount of resistance to that will change the fact of it. Remember Carl Jung's adage: *What you resist persists.* If you resist what is, you are creating suffering for yourself by ensuring its persistence. Now, I am *not* saying that you need to accept injustice, torture, pestilence and the like. Yes, our corporations are polluting the air and water, and, yes, this is harmful to our health. So, you don't resist what is *and* you speak out against injustice. This is perfectly logical if you think about it.

What is the non-dual perspective? Non-dualism recognizes that nothing is separate from me, that everything I experience is contained within me, that what affects others affects me and vice versa, and that consciousness is one field in which everything is contained. In a non-dual perspective, there is no comparison or judgment, like one thing is good and another is bad. There is just what *is*. This is why *Loving It All* makes so much sense, since it all is contained in my consciousness.

What does it mean to live with a non-dual perspective? It means accepting everything that comes with an awakened heart. Why? Because what comes is what you attracted with your thoughts and beliefs. Denying this and blaming circumstances on other people thereby disempowers you. By taking 100 percent responsibility for your world—no blame, no recrimination, no excuses—you experience real freedom in the midst of your world, and the joy that accompanies it!

Again, this is tricky to understand. I am *not* saying to blame the victim. Taken to its extreme, this could be interpreted as the victim bringing it all upon themselves and the perpetrators just obeying their wishes. Remember, your so-called outer world is just a reflection of your inner world. So, I am suggesting that you take 100 percent responsibility for your inner world, and the outer will reflect that perfectly. And, if it doesn't do that right away, you still can take 100 percent responsibility for your world as a way to empower yourself in that world.

This book is written along two parallel paths: (1) I will seek to show how the ego (or separate self) operates, the nature of dualistic mind, what the shadow is, the role of gratitude, service and living in the present moment as it relates to awakening, and an overall treatise on enlightenment and consciousness; and (2) I will use the spiritual tool called the Enneagram to show the nine types of egoic function and how to know your type and observe yourself operating with its habitual thoughts, feelings and behavior, and thereby be able to consciously decide to go another way—the way of freedom. In other words, this book will highlight a path for awakening the heart and using the Enneagram as a tool for awakening the consciousness.

I am writing the book this way to avoid what is so common with spiritual texts, namely, giving great spiritual principles without any tools to actually explore those principles in daily life. If you are willing to discover your Enneagram type, watch it as it takes hold in your consciousness and observe it operating from a conscious perspective, you are well on your way to an awakened consciousness. I want to give you the most useful tool I have found for self-observation and self-discovery: the Enneagram.

Throughout the book, I use the Enneagram to highlight the unconscious patterns of thought, feeling, and behavior that contribute to our worldwide mess. The modern-day Enneagram, based on an ancient geometric figure, describes nine fundamental personality styles (including their dominant thoughts, emotions and behaviors) and a spiritual path to awakening for each type. These Enneagram types are essentially archetypes of ego, the false identity formed as mankind sank into a dualistic consciousness.

The *passions* of each type (their habitual patterns of unconscious thought, belief and behavior that provide the motivational energy underlying the type itself) describe the different ways in which people sleepwalk through life. George I. Gurdjieff , the Persian mystic who is credited with bringing the Enneagram symbol to our Western shores in the early twentieth century, used the term *sleepwalking* to describe the semiconscious state in which most people live, reacting to their environment (being both in the world and of it, to use a biblical description) and being manipulated like puppets.

The word *enneagram* means nine-sided figure: *ennea* means nine and *grama* means figure. This symbol has been found in first-century churches as well as in ancient Sufi documents. Here is what it looks like:

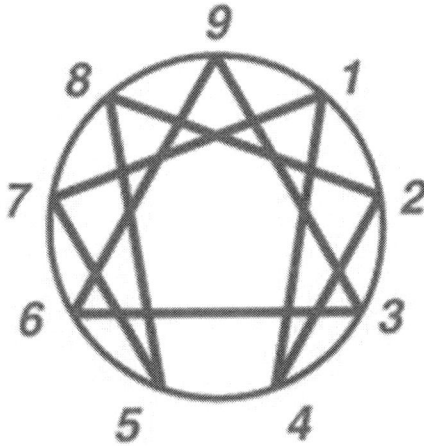

In the 1950s, Oscar Ichazo used this figure to map dimensions of personality. The nine points of the Enneagram depict nine different patterns of thinking, feeling and behaving, each with a different set of gifts and challenges. Each type has its own passion, fixation and virtue.

The passion is one's habitual stance of thought, feeling and behavior in the world. It could be called the negative aspect of the type; in fact, the passions are called by such names as sloth, deceit, gluttony, lust, fear, envy, avarice, pride and anger. The virtue is the healed and mature expression of that underlying passion. The fixation shows up when the type's natural tendency—"I *want* to..."—becomes "I *have* to..."; this means the tendency has become fixated in consciousness. For example, Type One's natural tendency is "I want to be good"; when this becomes a fixation, the Type One person feels pressured by the compulsion that "I *have* to be good." The Enneagram is a useful spiritual tool that can increase compassion and understanding toward yourself and toward others in your life.

The Peacemaker
9
The Challenger 8   **1 The Reformer**
The Enthusiast 7   **2 The Helper**
The Loyalist 6   **3 The Achiever**
The Investigator 5   **4 The Individualist**

The Enneagram with Riso-Hudson Type Names

These one-word descriptors can be expanded into four-word sets of traits. Keep in mind that these are merely highlights and do not represent the full spectrum of each type.

*Type **One** is principled, purposeful, self-controlled, and perfectionistic.*

*Type **Two** is generous, demonstrative, people-pleasing, and possessive.*

*Type **Three** is adaptable, excelling, driven, and image-conscious.*

*Type **Four** is expressive, dramatic, self-absorbed, and temperamental.*

*Type **Five** is perceptive, innovative, secretive, and isolated.*

*Type **Six** is engaging, responsible, anxious, and suspicious.*

*Type **Seven** is spontaneous, versatile, acquisitive, and scattered.*

*Type **Eight** is self-confident, decisive, willful, and confrontational.*

*Type **Nine** is receptive, reassuring, complacent, and resigned.*

Source: Don Riso and Russ Hudson, *The Wisdom of the Enneagram* (New York: Bantam Books, 1999), p. 8.

Each of the nine Enneagram types is more at home in, and processes information through, one of three *centers of intelligence*: the body (types Eight, Nine, and One), the heart or emotional realm (types Two, Three, and Four), or the mind (types Five, Six, and Seven). The Three-Six-Nine triad is the core of the Enneagram. The Three is the core emotional point; the Six, the core mental point; and the Nine, the core body point. Your Enneagram type is an indicator of how you organize your consciousness—whether you identify with your body, mind or emotions as the center of your consciousness.

What I like about the Enneagram is its effectiveness and versatility as a tool for self-inquiry and spiritual growth. As small children, we adopted survival strategies to help us cope with trauma and difficulty. These coping strategies stay with us into adulthood and become habits of thought and behavior. Understanding your Enneagram type can help you recognize habitual ways of thinking, feeling and acting that don't work for you anymore. They may have helped you survive childhood, and for that we can be thankful! But in adulthood, these habits of mind and behavior can cause trouble.

The Enneagram can also be of great assistance in healing a relationship. As you begin to see your partner from the perspective of their type, you may begin to understand why they do what they do. It isn't personal;

their behavior comes from their fixation, and your reaction to it stems from your own fixation. Understanding this reduces the emotional charge and helps you become more loving, accepting and compassionate toward your mate, rather than being constantly ticked off. You still might prefer that they act another way, but now, at least, you understand their habitual behavior, just as you are beginning to understand your own.

The Enneagram offers a practical system for transcending our ego identity. It is practical because you can use it right away to develop empathy for another person's point of view and their resultant behavior. And, perhaps more importantly, you can begin to observe your own unconscious patterns of behavior and consciously choose not to follow that well-worn path. The more you can observe your habitual behavior and choose anew, the closer you are to nondual consciousness. This is an extremely important point: by witnessing your habitual patterns of reaction, you observe them coming up, watch them as they position themselves in your consciousness, stay present, and just watch the passing show. If you don't get sucked into the drama of a particular pattern of reaction, it will pass on through. But if you react, you are caught in the trap of duality.

THE NINE ENNEAGRAM TYPES

As mentioned earlier, the nine points of the Enneagram system are built around three central points: the Nine (the passion or the motivator for the Nine is sloth), the Six (the passion is fear), and the Three (the passion is deceit). The Enneagram is arranged in three triads; the Eight-Nine-One triad is called the anger triad because the motivating force behind these types is anger, although they all express it differently. The Two-Three-Four triad is called the image triad since all of these types, as children, learn to adopt an image so they can feel loved (they are motivated to create an acceptable image). The Five-Six-Seven triad is called the fear triad since all three of these types are motivated by fear, although they express it quite differently.

Let's start with the Nine, the top point in the diagram. Paradoxically, this anger point is called the Peacemaker or the Mediator. It's hard to believe that Nines have underlying anger because they are so mellow and peaceable, but anger is their motivating force. Since they love peace, they can't let themselves express their anger, so they repress it.

How it shows up, then, is through the Nine "going to sleep," so to speak, living in the world in a slothful way. Nines simply check out when anger arises; they get lazy, off-purpose, and have difficulty making decisions. Presidents Ronald Reagan and Gerald Ford might be examples of the Nine fixation; it is said that First Lady Nancy Reagan (possibly a Two) made all the major decisions for Ronald and that he needed lots of naps!

Point Six, in contrast, is ruled by its passion of fear, which is also its motivating energy. The Six is referred to as the Loyal Skeptic—the result of the motivating force being expressed in the personality. Sixes are loyal and skeptical because they won't be OK or feel safe without being loyal to an authority figure (who will keep them feeling safe) and being skeptical (questioning everything). Sixes often think of what could go wrong, the worst possible scenario. They tend to be hyper-vigilant. They worry a lot; doubt and skepticism are their constant companions. The Six fixation causes a person to be extra careful with their children, for example, knowing that bad things do happen. Woody Allen is probably a classic Six.

The last of the core points, the Three (called the Performer or the Achiever), embodies the image motivation. Their passion is deceit; they are deceiving everyone to portray an image, including themselves! The fixation comes when they decide they *must* have an attractive image. The child learns early on that, to be loved and accepted, one must be a doer. Getting things done, being seen as successful, being busy all the time are hallmarks of this type. Extremely efficient and productive, Threes seek to promote that image to the world so that they can earn others' love and approval. Bill Clinton and Katie Couric may be classic Threes.

The other six types are interiorized and exteriorized versions of these three central types. The Eight (the Boss, Leader or Protector) is an overt (exteriorized) anger type; these folks can get mad, express it, and then be fine in five minutes (while everyone else is picking themselves up off the floor!). Their passion is lust; they want more of everything! Jack Nicholson probably is an Eight. The One (the Perfectionist) is also an anger type, but, since they seek to embody perfection, they can't get mad—it is not right or correct to show anger—so it comes out sideways as sarcasm, criticism, judgment, and constant attention to getting things right (according to their model of right and wrong). So, in addition to being their motivator, anger is also their passion. Clint Eastwood is probably a One. Think of one of his best movies, *The Unforgiven*—a classic One title, if there ever was one!

The exteriorized and interiorized versions of the fearful types (on either side of the Six in the Enneagram figure) are the Seven (the Epicure) and the Five (the Observer). The Seven doesn't look afraid at all. The passion of the Seven is gluttony, primarily gluttony for new experiences and adventures. Sevens are the optimists of the Enneagram, always looking for new, pleasant possibilities in the future. Robin Williams is probably a classic Seven. However, what propels them to constantly seek new adventures and stimulation is fear of pain, limitation, boredom and routine.

Fives are also fearful. Their passion is avarice; they hoard things, especially their information. They may have had a very intrusive parent who dominated them. They respond to stressful situations by pulling in so they can't be overwhelmed. Fives typically can't stand much social interaction without needing to recharge their batteries. Bob Dylan is probably a classic Five.

The Two (The Giver) is the exteriorized version of the Three. Their passion is pride; they believe "I am the best giver in the world!" Twos have learned that, to be loved, they must put others' needs over their own. John Travolta and Nancy Reagan are probably Twos. A good look at the Two in action is the female lead (played by an actual Two, Elizabeth Shue) in the movie *Leaving Las Vegas*. Shue's character is like a chameleon, looking to fill whatever need Nicholas Cage's character might have. The Two style is to become what the other person wants them to become in serving their needs.

The Four is the interiorized version of the Three. The Four (the Tragic Romantic) tends to see their life as missing something important, and feels envious of others who seem to have what the Four lacks. Their passion is envy. This is not jealousy—they do not want to take away what you have; they just wish they had it, too! Fours can be melancholic and are usually unique individuals (often artistic). Angst and drama often mark the life of a Four. Jim Morrison of the Doors and Judy Garland were probably classic Fours.

The system is more complicated, though, than simply nine personality types. Since this typology is cross-cultural, and all seven billion of us theoretically fit into types One through Nine, there is obviously a lot of variation within types. Each individual usually has a dominant *wing* (the numbers to the left and right of the type on the circle) that influences the expression of their main type. So, for example, a Nine can have a One or Eight wing; this means their laziness can be modified by overt anger (Eight) or by a critical attitude toward themselves and their world (One).

Each type is also expressed though one of three instinctual subtypes. These subtypes are called (1) *self-preservation*, a tendency to focus on physical and material security; (2) *social*, a tendency to join groups, network, and be concerned with being a group member and fitting in;

and (3) *relational* or *sexual*, tending to want intimate, close relationships with a few people. So, for example, a sexual Seven would express their excitement for positive, future possibilities (the passion of the Seven is gluttony) and through their strong desire for close, intimate relationships with others. Again, the passion is the energy that infuses the type's expression in the world, and the fixation is where the person locks into "I *have* to be this way!"

Each type also tends to move toward two other types in certain situations. They go toward one type when they are feeling stressed and toward another when they are feeling secure. Sevens, for example, move toward or act more like a One (the critical, judgmental perspective) when under stress, and they move to the Five (the observer who loves knowledge and being the expert) when they're feeling comfortable.

This is a complex typology. As one learns the system, one can see how one is habitually acting in a predictable way with others. The best way I have found to learn the system is through the use of panels. Here a group of people who share the same basic type—say, for example, they're all Fives—get up in front of the observers and are interviewed by a facilitator about what it is like to be a Five. The ensuing conversation is very revealing! This also serves to develop empathy; when you hear stories from a group of people about what it is like to have a particular type, you can suddenly wake up to the why of a particular friend's behavior.

Through this system there is much that we can learn about ourselves, about our relationships with others and, ultimately, about our spiritual growth into whole, compassionate beings. This system allows you to have increased empathy and compassion for yourself and for others.

Let me use my marriage as an example. My wife is a self-preservation Nine with a One wing. A person trained in the system would know that, as a Nine, she has *anger* as her core motivating force. But, since her personality orientation is the Mediator (the name of the Nine ego type), she is mostly unwilling to show the anger. Why? Because anger can cause conflict and the Nine wants to avoid conflict at all costs! Therefore she represses it so that she can be nice to others, care for others, and help to smooth ruffled feathers. Once in a great while, she will explode with anger, but it is rare.

Another aspect of the Nine type is that their characteristic passion or vice is *sloth*. It takes so much energy to keep the anger repressed that the Nine often gets lazy and unfocused as a result. They fall asleep to their own needs and purpose in life, looking instead to please others and serve them. The Nine child was typically invisible in the family of origin (they felt their needs were unimportant and therefore ignored) and, as a way to survive, they began to help others and put their own needs aside (so as to stay in the background).

My wife's One *wing* (the Perfectionist) modifies her Nine tendencies; it shows up as a concern to get things done right according to her understanding of correctness. Her instinctual *subtype* is self-preservation, which means her focus is on her own material and physical security and comfort; she is concerned with nutrition, exercise, her home environment, and so forth.

By contrast, I am a sexual-subtype Seven with an Eight wing. This means my motivator is fear and my personality type is the Epicure. I am interested in things that are new, exciting, spontaneous, interesting, fun, and so on. What I fear most is pain and/or boredom. I love to sample life in every aspect; what is challenging for me is to stick with something after it loses its newness and excitement. My Eight wing (the Boss) helps me be decisive and a leader; this alone allows me to complete things that a Seven with a Six wing might have more trouble with. My characteristic passion or vice is gluttony, primarily a gluttony for experience. The Seven child typically deals with fearful issues by constantly moving, trying new things, as a way to avoid feeling pain. My instinctual subtype is sexual (also called relational); this means that I want to connect deeply with others. Superficial relationships are not of much interest to me.

With this brief review, you can perhaps see some of the challenges we have experienced in our marriage. My wife's Nine type loves security, home, predictability, comfort, and is indecisive; my Seven type wants to travel, try new things, take risks, make impulsive decisions, have fun. She experiences my impulsivity as flightiness; I have thought that she can be a stick-in-the-mud.

Another potential source of conflict is my extroversion; when we are out together, while I am excited to connect with others (my sexual sub-type), she is embarrassed at being thrust into the spotlight with me. She prefers to stay in the background and continue to serve others. I can be an embarrassment to her. Sevens are also self-referent, which means that I look primarily after my own needs, while she, as a Nine, doesn't typically know what her needs are! She might get mad at me for being selfish, while I get irritated with her slothful lack of purpose, her constant helping others and not being herself. Finally, her One wing (the Perfectionist) grates on my Seven type, which is free-wheeling and fun-loving. I can experience her as uptight, and she can experience me as sloppy and impulsive. I see her perfectionism as limiting, and the Seven hates limits!

This all sounds sort of negative, but obviously each type also has its strengths. My wife is wonderfully empathetic by nature; I have to work at it (being primarily self-referent). Her concern for home and hearth leads her to create a beautiful, tranquil environment for us to live in. And although she seems subdued in contrast to me, she does like adventure. The perfectionist in her notices important details that I completely miss, and she points out things that I didn't see in my haste to get one thing done and move on to the next. Similarly, my "flightiness" as a Seven can also be seen as bringing spontaneity, excitement, optimism, and a sense of fun to our life together. My love of intimacy helps me stay committed to our marriage. Her self-preservation tendency helps her focus on nutrition, exercise and health, which serves both of us well.

By understanding the tendencies of each type with its wing, its subtype and its movement to other types, you can see that what your partner, friend, or spouse is doing has nothing to do with you personally. They are just operating within the framework that's natural to their type. So you learn to view what they do with a bemused smile rather than defensive reaction. My wife and I have been married 30 years, and our struggles have largely disappeared since I began my study of the Enneagram. Now we are often able to simply smile with understanding when either of us acts in an egoic manner. Being the observer (the witness) of the habitual behavior lessens its strength to elicit reactive behavior in either of us. And this, ultimately, is a step toward a non-dualistic life.

There are many excellent books that can give you a more complete overview of this system. I recommend beginning with either of these two: Riso and Hudson, *The Wisdom of the Enneagram*; or Daniels and Price, *The Essential Enneagram.*

I hope you enjoy the ride that this book will take you on. It is an invitation to live fully in your wholeness, and to let the ego fade into that oneness and be integrated into the Self you truly are: a spiritual being with unlimited potential and grace.

CHAPTER 1

♡

What Is Love?

The Guest House

This being human is a guest house.
Every morning a new arrival.

A joy, a depression, a meanness,
some momentary awareness comes
as an unexpected visitor.

Welcome and entertain them all!
Even if they're a crowd of sorrows,
who violently sweep your house
empty of its furniture,
still, treat each guest honorably.
He may be clearing you out
for some new delight.

The dark thought, the shame, the malice,
meet them at the door laughing,
and invite them in.

Be grateful for whoever comes,

Because each has been sent
as a guide from beyond.

—Rumi

"Love . . . is our ultimate reality and our purpose on earth. To be consciously
aware of it, to experience love in ourselves and others, is the meaning of life."
—Marianne Williamson, *A Return to Love*

What is love? Poets and artists of all stripes have pondered this question for eons. Different types of love have been described, including *agape*, the purest form of love. But what *is* it? Is it a feeling, an energy, a substance? Can you fall in love or out of love? Why does love seem so elusive, so fragile?

One answer is that you can't define love. It is a mysterious force which seems to be central to the unfolding of the universe. However, we humans like to define things, so here's my attempt at a definition: *Love is the binding force of the universe, that which holds all life in a divine design so that creative intelligence can work its magic.*

Didn't expect that, did you? Sound kind of impersonal and unemotional? However, it is a marvel and a revelation if you really understand that statement. Universal love is actually what unites us in our apparent differences. Factually, we are united, heart to heart, in this universal love. This current of love is the electromagnetic energy that binds all sentient life together in union. But, if this is so, why do things seem to be separate and different in our perception?

The apparent separation is a result of the human mind. We learn, soon after birth, that most things are outside of us and separate from us. We learn that we have to depend on these outside factors for our sustenance and, yes, survival. The first such outside factor is usually our mother. This is where what is called *conditional love* begins. We *need* our mother to feed us and care for us. So we begin to develop strategies to "win" that love. If we are "good," we receive love; if we are "bad" (according to social convention), love is apparently withheld and/or punishment ensues. Thus begins what has been called the *socialization process*. We learn very quickly what we need to do and how we need to act in order to "win" love. At this early age when we are so dependent on our mother, we learn these lessons very quickly.

THE HUMAN SHADOW

This is where the *human shadow* gets formed. Carl Jung, Robert Bly and many others have spoken of the shadow, and there are numerous "shadow work" seminars in today's human potential movement. The shadow is essentially all the parts of ourselves that get repressed or shoved into the unconscious because they are unacceptable to those upon whom we depend for love. They don't go away, though; they are still inside us and able to wreak havoc on our perception of reality.

All of this shadow material gets projected out into the so-called real world so that enemies and "bad" people seem to appear. This, of course, is the main source of conflict in the world. We are constantly trying to get rid of all those "bad folks out there" who are causing us grief. But most people are blissfully unaware that they are creating their own reality and what they create is colored by their shadow elements. Thus, people are often reacting to their own creations as though they are completely "out there."

The human *ego* is what could be called the "mind-made self." The ego consists of all the beliefs, attitudes and values we have formed, since birth, that serve as our navigation system for life on earth. Part of this ego self is the shadow. This small, limited self is actually a false self; it is not who we really are. Who we really are is our universal self, the self that is made of unconditional love. The ego knows nothing of unconditional love; in fact, the ego cannot love unconditionally. Why? Because the ego depends upon resistance to *what is* as the way it continues to survive.

The ego is never content with what is; it wants to change it, improve it, make it more comfortable for itself…all manner of things *except* acceptance as it is. In this way, it convinces itself that it can be in control of things. Its resistance comes from two possible sources: (1) the past—the ego views the present situation through the lens of the past and interprets it as a threat or possible enhancement to itself; or (2) the future—the ego sees the situation as a possible threat or enhancement to itself based on an imaginary future. If the person stays in the present moment and loves the situation unconditionally, the ego has no "juice" or energy to keep itself going.

The primary motivation of the ego is to maintain a separate self; this is the false identity we all know and operate from. The ego depends on a separate identity; without this, it fears that it would disappear into the truth of Oneness. But let me be very clear about one thing here; what we see and experience as the external world is *not* the true reality that exists. It is a mind-made reality composed of our projections of our internal state. So the separated self creates a reality which it then reacts to, thereby strengthening itself as separate from the outer world. Hence, we have likes and dislikes, opinions, and so on. This is all conditional depending on who we like and who we don't like. If we suddenly became unconditionally loving to everyone, the ego would protest mightily.

But, when we identify with the ego as our self, then we act out of conditional love. That is, we love those people who conform to our expectations and desires, and we withhold love from those who don't. Think about this metaphor: the sun shines its light on all beings, not just the ones it likes or approves of. Unconditional love is like that—it shines on everyone and has no preferences regarding what it does and doesn't like.

So, to summarize, we build up an ego in an attempt to protect ourselves from those so-called bad things outside of us, when in fact those bad things are a projection of our shadow elements and of the ego itself. When a group of people have been conditioned this way, we have a collective phenomenon called *consensual reality*. We all agree that bad things seem to happen all the time…even to so-called good people! This often gets translated as meaning that God is angry with us (by people with a religious proclivity). Here is where the ill effects of religion come into play. Assuming that there are bad people out there, religions have formulated a set of do's and don'ts (such as the Ten Commandments) to help us be good people. This conditioning from the past is very strong and it is the source of much misery. The notion of sin is also a projection of the human ego since it (the ego) wants to judge good and bad.

Life happens in the moment. With strong conditioning from the past, we learn to *react* to situations according to certain preformed rules and principles rather than *respond* to them uniquely as they occur. When you react to any situation, it is often the wrong thing to do because it is based on the past, not the present circumstance. Think of the word *re-sponsibility*. We can think of it as response-ability: the ability to respond. When one operates from the consciousness rooted in the present moment, rather than obeying past conditioning, then one responds to the current situation as it is, without the colorings of the past. This is what is desirable: to respond to any situation as if it were brand new. And it is brand new—this moment has never occurred before.

Conditioned reactions are created by the fragile human ego. In fact, some religions have been created to explain "bad" reality as being caused by a wrathful deity. The Old Testament of the Bible is full of statements about a wrathful God. Unconditional love would never create such a reality. And unconditional love is in fact the nature of God or Spirit. Unconditional love is seeking to unite us in our so-called differences. Unconditional love *is* God! Only the fearful ego would make up such phenomena as conditional love and "bad" people. By projecting our fears and shadow elements out into the world and then blaming a wrathful God for this, we get to avoid taking personal responsibility for the world we have collectively created.

DEALING WITH OUR SHADOW

What is the path out of this bind? Well, for one thing, we need to allow this repressed material of the shadow out of the unconscious so it can be *felt* and allowed to integrate into our conscious awareness. This can be a painful process as these old hurts gets activated. Some people might say "Well, if I feel it fully, I might go kill someone!" This won't happen because what makes you want to kill someone is repressed anger, not anger that you just feel and stay steady with. If you are willing to just feel the anger deeply then it will be released. The alternative is that if we are unwilling to do this work, the anger will stay repressed in our unconscious and continue to wreak havoc in our worlds.

One technique I have found to be useful is journaling. When I get activated by some old hurt, I sit down and ask myself, "What must I believe in order for this to be activated?" Then I write down what comes to mind. If I am willing to be totally honest, an answer will come. Then, I *feel* that belief (and its attendant emotional charge) and allow it to change. Again, there is a fear that, if I feel my anger deeply, I might hurt someone. I might get angrier and angrier. But that doesn't happen; anger builds up

7

because it is *not* felt fully. It is projected "out there" towards someone you imagine is causing the anger in you. But "out there" is "in here." There is nothing out there that is not also in your inner experience. This seems counterintuitive but nonetheless is true.

Many beliefs we have formed are not actually true, but come from one or more of these painful childhood traumas; by examining the belief, we can see if it is true. If it is not true, we can let it go. If you adopt the standpoint of a detached *observer* of your reactions, they are freed of their pent-up energy and this allows great creative energy to be released...which had been bound up inside you, protecting you from feeling the "bad" stuff. Freeing up the energy that's been boxed up in your shadow is essential for your creativity and, perhaps more importantly, for you being able to perceive the world as it actually is.

For example, maybe we were told by a significant person in our life that we were stupid, and we accepted their statement as true. Beliefs tend to have a self-fulfilling quality. If we believe we are stupid, we will act in such a way as to prove that this is true. One experiment done years ago used a classroom with students who had identical IQ scores. Half the class members were told by the teacher that they were slow learners and would be given special tutoring to catch them up with the others. The other half were told they were very smart and were expected to perform at a high level. At the end of the term, the so-called "slow learners" were performing at a much lower level than the other students in the class...and yet they all had the same IQ! This illustrates the fact that we see what we expect to see (or are told to see).

THERE IS NO "OUT THERE" OUT THERE!

The point is this: the so-called problem is *never* out there. We are all connected by universal love, so there is no "out there" out there! We are all part of a living, dynamic whole. Everything we experience is a projection of our inner landscape, which is strongly colored by our old hurts and traumas. We need to embody *all* aspects of ourselves; we need to welcome it all! Hence, the title of this book, *Loving It All*. When we can welcome everything that comes to us without resisting anything, we are on the way to freedom.

To repeat, the ego maintains itself by *resistance to what is*. This resistance comes from the old wounding (shadow) and it seems logical, given the colored reality we perceive with the shadow intact. Carl Jung said something that really rings true here: *What you resist persists*. But when you accept life as it is, a tremendous sense of freedom will rise up in you. You are no longer being controlled by your past conditioning and are free to choose your response in any given situation.

As long as we are unwilling to face our hurts and trauma, we will never live in a peaceful world. All the laws, governmental agencies, police or armies in the world will not move us into peace if we don't take on the task of *feeling* all aspects of ourselves. Feeling the darkness is the quickest way of doing this. But, if we continue to deny this shadow, it will continue to wreak havoc and all the outer forms, like laws, courts, police, and so on, will at best be only a holding action against the darkness.... which is, in reality, in ourselves! Laws, courts, and police are a logical manifestation of the egoic reality; it does *look* like a dangerous world out there. But what if "bad" people were just severely wounded souls with lots of shadow elements inside? Wouldn't psychiatric care seem a more logical response? Putting people in prison with more wounded people simply teaches people to be more "bad"!

Another technique I have found to be extremely useful to observing the shadow in action is the psycho-spiritual technology called the Enneagram. The Enneagram is a personality typology that identifies nine distinct ways of feeling, thinking and behaving. Once you discover your type, you can begin to observe yourself acting and thinking in habitual ways common to that type. For example, I am a type Seven, which tends to fear boredom and pain. Sevens therefore tend to "future-trip" to avoid both. They tend to be impulsive and extroverted in order to cover up a deeper sense of unworthiness. We Sevens are adventurous, optimistic, gregarious and spontaneous; we tend to see the world with "rose-colored glasses," thereby missing some actual things that need our attention. The passion of the Seven is gluttony; we tend to be gluttons for experience. Anything new and potentially exciting, we are drawn to. Our spiritual path, therefore, consists of learning to stay in the present moment (and foregoing "future-tripping") and practicing sobriety (tempering our addiction to excitement by saying no to some things that might have seduced us in the past).

The Seven's fixation is *not* my true identity; all types are merely ego types formed at birth (in the DNA, by the latest behavioral research) and solidified by trauma and hurt. They are basically survival mechanisms against the so-called outer world and, while perhaps useful in our early years, must be integrated into our full awareness in order for us to heal completely. Each of the nine types has certain strengths and weaknesses, but in the end it is still the false self seeking wholeness where it cannot be found—in the illusory outer world. The beauty of the Enneagram system is that, once you know your type, you can begin to observe yourself "doing your type" and consciously choose a non-habitual and non-conditioned response. In other words, you now have conscious volition instead of conditioned, habitual reaction.

LOVING UNCONDITIONALLY

The so-called outer world is fraught with illusory perceptions made by people who have unhealed shadow elements in their consciousness (see Chapter 3 for more on this). This would include most of us! We don't see clearly because our wounds and hurts are distorting our perception of what is actually present. So an attitude that whatever seems to be happening in the outer world does not matter to me is very helpful. If we can remain unattached to what seems to be going on in the outer world, and just maintain an attitude of gratitude, then tranquility is maintained. What is needed is a steadfast detachment towards the unreal in the recognition that the mind is constantly distorting what seems to be out there.

What you love is right there in front of you, but you must see it with the eyes of the heart. How can we do this? Parker Palmer has some good suggestions on this. For one thing, we can stop trying to give advice, fix the other person, save them or set them straight. This is *not* loving communication. Instead, we can *allow* the other person to just be the way they are. We can speak our own truth without making the other person "wrong." We can stop interrupting the other person with what *we* want to say. We can ask honest, open questions with *no* agenda in mind—in other words, we don't know the answer to the question and we ask it with genuine curiosity. We can offer silence if we have nothing to say. We can laugh at our own foibles. And we can stop asking "expert" questions to try and "one-up" the other person.

Here are some examples of closed questions (which have an agenda, hidden or not): "Did you think about talking to a counselor?" "Will you be getting a job right after you graduate?" "Are you keeping up with your homework?" "Can I mention this to your boss?" Some examples of expert questions to avoid are: "Don't you think...?" "Wouldn't you agree...?" "Isn't it true that...?" "Aren't you saying...?" "Why didn't you...?" All these can be egoic questions designed to direct the person in the way you think they should go, which may not have relevance to the reality of what they're experiencing. Open questions might be "What do you think you might do after you graduate?" or "Would you be willing to share with me what you are considering?"

The mind alone can never see reality as it is because its machinations are constantly colored by the dictates of the society, your religion, your parents, and other so-called authorities. When you can't see that love is your nature, you are allowing the mind, and its addiction to fear and lack, to rule your perception. If you depend on your mind for your construction of reality, you are doomed to a life of ups and downs, of pain and pleasure, of despair and happiness...but rarely contentment and bliss. An integrated heart (with all shadow elements healed and blessed) can only see love. True love, then, is the capacity to see the light that has been shrouded by the darkness. And this we call the *awakened heart*. You are then seeing reality with the heart, not the mind.

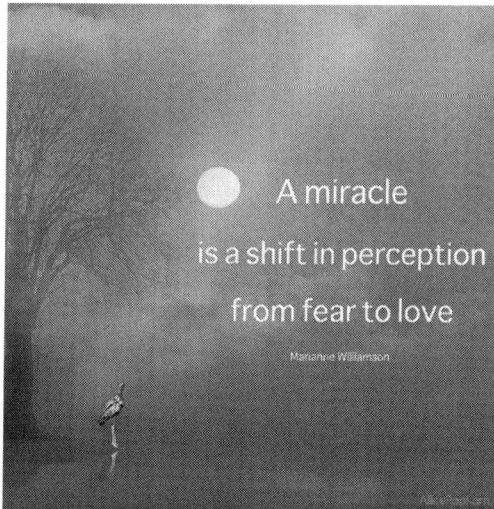

A miracle
is a shift in perception
from fear to love

Marianne Williamson

TWO EMOTIONS: FEAR AND LOVE

There are only two primary emotions and many variants of each: fear and love. Fear is a contractive emotion; it comes from unhealed trauma and causes one to shrink smaller and smaller in identity. Examples of fear-based emotions are anger, jealousy, hatred, resentment and guilt.

Love, on the other hand, causes one to expand into one's true identity as a creator. Love shows up as appreciation, gratitude, acceptance, generosity and kindness. For a peaceful world that is actually whole, we need to express the qualities of love into our world on a continuous basis.

Here, again, we see the power of consensual reality. If enough of us begin to live from this expanded reality, a sort of "hundredth monkey" effect (a term coined by Lyall Watson) is created. This is best explained by biologist Rupert Sheldrake's morphogenetic field theory, which postulates that if enough members of a certain type of sentient life begin seeing things radically differently—in this case, with the eyes of love— all of that life-form will then become resonant with that perspective.

Find the Self who is worthy of all that you really are: your true Self. Release your doubts, your guilt, your feelings of being undeserving, and learn to accept. Train yourself to maintain the focus on your desired future and welcome it with gratitude, and that energy alone will at last allow it to come to you. Since we are the creators of our personal reality, if we see with the eyes of fear, then we will experience a dangerous world.

Planet Earth has been gripped by this fear ethos for millennia. And why, do you suppose, is this true? Because egoic people hungry for power to assuage their basic sense of helplessness (caused by letting their minds, disconnected from the source of life, rule) always seek power over others to feel safe. Remember this: the mind is *always* insecure since it is operating on an untrue premise—that it is separate from its Source and therefore it needs to control and/or predict reality so it can stay safe. But life is basically a grand adventure, not a brutish, short thing to be endured.

THE ENNEAGRAM PERSPECTIVE ON LOVE

The Enneagram type Nine is the type that really focuses on love as its principal point of orientation. However, because the Nine tends to avoid conflict, suppress its anger, distract itself to avoid feeling the anger, see all points of view but miss its own, and typically does not know what it wants, a Nine person feels far away from love. But as Nines become more awake and present to themselves, they will become aware of their absence of contact with their essential nature and the need to remedy this. Because they have focused their attention on where others are coming from and thereby felt invisible in their world, they tend to feel deficient, unloved, unimportant and overlooked. They typically felt invisible in their family system because they learned, early on, that to avoid conflict (their chief goal) and stay out of the way, they needed to be "invisible." However, since their gift is seeing other points of view very easily, if they can also honor and love *themselves*, they will, at long last, know themselves as a manifestation and embodiment of the love of the Divine.

A HISTORICAL PERSPECTIVE

Finally, let us examine a historical perspective on all this. I think we can all agree that a renaissance of Divine Love is what is needed. The ego's domination is nearing an end as all societal systems built on its dominance (read: fear-based systems) are failing. Let us look back to the first Renaissance that transformed the planet some 500 years ago in Florence, Italy. In the middle of the fourteenth century, humanity was living in the Dark Ages and our affinity for culture and the arts was practically nonexistent. Then there was a renaissance of right-brain thinking, representing the Divine Feminine (the right brain processes art, beauty, intuition, nurturance and cooperation, among other things, which are typically seen as feminine virtues), and arts and culture flourished.

As the Renaissance progressed, the wisdom embodied in the arts and culture penetrated the consciousness of folks living at that time. As this sacred knowledge filtered into humanity's hearts and minds, art, music, dance, literature and every other creative facet of the Renaissance elevated people to a new level of culture and civility. This Renaissance played a large role in liberating the human mind as people began to pull away from the oppressive control of the Church. This marked a momentous turning point in history. There was a resurgence in the human spirit that made possible all the modern achievements of humanity. It initiated an atmosphere that was favorable to new ideas, innovative accomplishments and creativity in every endeavor.

The most amazing part of this was that this transformation was accomplished in the middle of the Dark Ages, at a time when human egos were manipulating minds and hearts, a time when humanity was truly asleep. Sadly, it seems we have regressed in recent years as the forces of left-brain, rational thought devoid of connection to the heart have pummeled the arts, and have substituted mindless TV, video games and consumerism. It is past time for a new renaissance—a renaissance of the heart-based thinking that will transform the world once again. And it is occurring: millions of people are now awake or are awakening to the evidence of dark control forces that have been manipulating us for quite a while. (See the movie *Thrive* for more on this theme.) We are beginning to feel again; we are beginning to allow the Divine Design of Life to manifest through our consciousness and, literally, to "let go and let God" control our thoughts, emotions and behavior.

IN SUMMARY

Harry Palmer, creator of the Avatar® seminars, put it this way: "When you adopt the viewpoint that there is nothing that exists that is not part of you, that there is no one who exists who is not part of you, that any judgment you make is self-judgment, that any criticism you level is self-criticism, you will wisely extend to yourself an unconditional love that will be the light of the world."

CHAPTER 2

The Curse of Duality

"Changes in life are always going to happen; they're part of the human experience. What we can change, however, is how we perceive them. And that shift in our perception is a miracle."
—Marianne Williamson, *A Return to Love: Reflections on the Principles of* A Course in Miracles

It should be clear to you now that duality is the state of consciousness from which you and I operate. What is duality? It is the perception that you are here and everything else is out there, separate from you. This illusion is very convincing to the mind since that is where it is created and projected into the so-called outer world. As the Course in Miracles points out, the body is the really convincing piece of evidence you have to show you how separate you are.

Because of this appearance of separation, it constantly appears that others are doing things to you, either so-called positive or negative things. This is the cause of our reactions to events. We are firmly convinced that others (or situations) are "doing it to us." It looks like others are hurting us, judging us, belittling us, and so on. But what is really happening?

What is happening is that parts of our consciousness are being projected out there to show us where we have unhealed places in ourselves.

If it wasn't inside us at all, it would not show up out there. Remember, everything is connected and it is all *one thing*. So when there appears to be something outside us that we don't like, the correct solution is to love it without judgment. Now, this runs counter to your instinct which says "they can't do this to me," "I don't deserve to be treated this way," and so forth. But if in fact we are all part of God, and God is love, and God is everything, then how can one part of God harm another part? It makes no sense logically, does it? Anything that is not love, not God, is fear, and fear is "**f**alse **e**vidence **a**ppearing **r**eal." I love that acronym because this is the truth of the matter.

I had an experience of this internal-projection-out-there recently when I went to help a friend with her work. I was still feeling pretty bad from a bout of stomach flu, but I went anyway to support her. Before I knew it, she was yelling at me because I didn't want to stay too long. She didn't thank me for coming, for supporting her at all; I just got criticized for leaving too soon because she apparently had expected that I would stay for a while. Boy, did I feel like a victim! Here I was, trying to help a friend, and apparently getting kicked in the teeth for my trouble! But when I allowed the emotion to clear, I saw that I was not unconditionally loving to her. I had wanted her to appreciate my effort; in other words, I had conditions on my love.

If you can agree on the fact of Oneness (even if you still experience the separated state of "me" and "them"), you will be able to agree that the idea of one part of God hurting another part of God is a ludicrous thought! If we are to remember who we really are, a part of the Divine whole, then we will have to release ourselves from the trance of duality. And it is factually a trance. We are all caught in its spell.

It is one thing to know with our minds that we are part of God; it is quite another thing to know it to the core of our being. And how do we get there? By noticing, from the observer position of objectivity, that what seems to happen to us from the so-called outside environment is merely a product of a projected unhealed part of ourselves. Easier said than done! But it is the only way I know to traverse the walk from the curse of duality to the joy of knowing the truth of Oneness. Basically, what is happening is that you are undergoing a reunion with yourself, a re-joining of parts of yourself that have split off in an attempt to experience what is it like to be separate from Source.

I have had the experience of Oneness and it is unmistakable; I saw that what appeared to be "out there" was really contained within *me*. I was in a seminar called Avatar and was doing a process called "Feel Its." In this process, you look at something—a tree, for example—and penetrate it with your consciousness, extending that penetration to the roots, the limbs, the back, all of it. Then, you can actually *feel* what it feels like to be a tree. Implausible as this may sound, you can do it. I have also done this with a seagull and I could feel the wind under my wings, my little heart beating in my chest, and the glory of what I saw from above the earth. When you experience this enough, you begin to see that everything is part of *you*.

A BAD HABIT

We are slaves to a bad habit, really—this idea that we are separate from each other and from all life. And this bad habit is causing us more and more grief as years pass. By believing that we are separate from all life and then acting that out, we find ourselves isolated and seemingly alone, with nothing but our egos to keep us safe. And everyone knows that egos do a terrible job of that, since they are based on fear in the first place! Egos are afraid all the time, because being at odds with the pulsations of the universe (the creative juice that animates everything that is alive), out of harmony with the life force, is a scary place to be. This habit is so old that we literally have forgotten that we are *one* with everything—the earth, the animals, reptiles, insects...all of it. And yet, we are beginning to remember. We can clearly see that the world of duality we experience with our senses is a mad world, completely insane, upside down, really. And, even though it is familiar, it is *not* our true home.

RETURNING HOME

We are seeking to return to our Source, back to our true identity. Years ago, I was part of a spiritual group that taught these truths—that we are all One, and so forth. And I had a mental understanding of that truth. But a surface mental understanding is obviously not sufficient! We are moving into a state where we are much more than what we thought we were in this temporary and delusional state of duality. Millennia ago, we dropped from a state of Oneness into the duality consciousness and began to see everything as separate from us. Who knows? Maybe we needed to do this for some reason like, perhaps, to experience what it would be like to be separate from Source? But we did do it; this is what has been called the "fall from grace" in the Christian Bible. Up until now, we have experienced ourselves as small, vulnerable bodies subject to all manner of harm, living in a dangerous, sometimes hostile world. In the egoic state of duality, everything seems big and overwhelming to us; in the expanded state of Oneness, we can begin to see ourselves as part of a giant fabric of creation.

When humanity "fell from grace" some eons ago, we dropped in vibration from a multidimensional awareness (the so-called Garden of Eden experience) into a three-dimensional universe of duality perceived with our five senses and interpreted by our minds: right/wrong, good/bad, light/dark, hot/cold, loud/quiet, soft/hard, smelly/fragrant, happy/unhappy, and so on. Once we decided that polarities exist, we then decided to judge some as "good" and some as "bad." The Bible put it this way: we chose to eat the fruit of the Tree of the

Knowledge of Good and Evil rather than of the Tree of Life. Once we decided to eat of this tree, duality was created. We now seem to have run the duality program about as far as we can go; our politics are divisive, racism has not healed, sexism still rears its ugly head, and so on. Duality is a necessary product of the human ego. Think of it this way: duality is created by the ego, which means separation from Source. This is why the ego is so fearful. It is frightening to be separated from your Source, from God.

One thing about the ego that you need to understand: the ego thrives on *resistance to what is*. Why does it do this? Because the ego lives in constant fear of ceasing to exist, so it feels threatened by what is happening (or might happen). Judgment is its way of being ready for danger. In other words, the ego is in a stance of opposition to what is. Just accepting life as it shows up is *not* what the ego is looking for. It is looking to judge, criticize, complain; this strengthens the ego identity.

Accepting and loving it all is what weakens the ego. That is why the title of this book is *Loving It All*. By doing this, you drop that poisonous fruit out of your mouth (to go back to the biblical metaphor). Remember that quote at the end of Chapter 1: "When you adopt the viewpoint there is nothing that exists that is not part of you...." Here is the way out of duality; it is called the non-dual perspective, and many writers (Ken Wilber, Jeff Foster, Eckhart Tolle, Byron Katie, etc.) now are picking up on this theme.

So, if we are all part of *one whole*, then why don't we experience ourselves that way? We cannot perceive our oneness with all life because, as Ken Wilber puts it in his book *Grace and Grit*, our "awareness is clouded and obstructed by...the activity of contracting and focusing awareness on my personal self or ego. My awareness is not open, relaxed, and God-centered, it is closed, contracted, and self-centered. And precisely because I am identified with the self-contraction..., I can't find or discover my prior identity, my true identity, with the All. My individual nature...

is thus fallen"—again using the biblical metaphor—living "in sin and separation and alienation from Spirit and from the rest of the world." When we live in this condition, our identity "seems completely boxed up and imprisoned in this isolated wall of mortal flesh."

This is what duality is. We see ourselves as the "subject" and everything outside of us as the "object." Wilber goes on to say that "the self-contraction"—the self-centeredness—the subject/object dualism, cannot perceive reality as it is…. Sin [or separation] is not something the self *does*, it is something the self *is*." The word *sin* comes from a root word meaning "to miss the mark," which is exactly what this self-contraction does: we miss reality in exchange for a mind-made world composed of a projection of our internal beliefs, attitudes and values *about* reality.

MORE ABOUT DUALITY

Duality produces a number of not-so-helpful phenomena for you. One, it re-creates the past. As you will note in Chapter 6, "The Present Moment," the past is a mind-made fiction. Many experiments have been done on the inaccuracy of memory. Your memory is inaccurate because the way you envision the past is simply a thought-form that you have stored away to refer to as you create your present reality. What you think of as the past is actually a result of using the stored mental files to create your mind-made world in the present! The same thing is true of the future; it does not exist, either. It is a mind-made fantasy and it contains such thought-forms as anticipation, expectation, and so on. All of these thoughts have accompanying emotions attached to them. So some people fear the future while others anticipate the future with delight. But it is all mind-stuff!

The only time that is real is the *present moment.* In the present moment, there is a perfect letting go to the inner guide, the God within. One ceases to want anything or to be averse to anything because there are no beliefs about reality in the present. So there is no effort to strive, climb the social ladder, struggle for a reward, avoid an undesirable outcome, and so on. In the present, one rightly just allows the inner urge, the God within, to direct one's actions.

There are some other consequences for adopting a dualistic perspective. Some of these are judgment, pain, emotional upset, jealousy, comparison, and feeling small and insignificant, to name a few. Also, there is always the temptation, in duality, to seek punishment for those who apparently harm us. This is the source of our judicial system. But, as I pointed out earlier, blaming one part of your body for doing something to you is really ludicrous.

I believe duality is becoming obsolete for our planet. How in the world can I say this with all the evidence of disintegration around us?

Political parties fighting, families quarrelling, people in the street protesting...the "evidence" seems to be of more duality, not less. Yes, the consensual reality created by ego-dominated humans is producing a fragmented, fearful world. Yet, if you look closely, you can see the emerging signs of unity; folks helping out after Hurricane Sandy, spontaneous gifting at Christmas to total strangers, random acts of kindness and charity all around, and so on. How is this happening? It is all about frequency and vibration.

All energy vibrates; lower-level vibrations produce dense material and higher levels produce less dense matter. The same is true of consciousness. Higher-vibration consciousness produces more peace, harmony and unity; read David Hawkins' pioneering work of *Power vs. Force* (Carlsbad, CA: Hay House, 2012). Also, look at the work from Maharishi University in Fairfield, Iowa; their experiments show that when there are a significant number of meditators in an area, crime goes down significantly. Here is the "good" news: as more and more people vibrate at higher levels of consciousness, since we are all part of *one whole*, the vibrational level of the whole goes up, because higher vibrations have more power than lower ones, according to Hawkins.

MOVING INTO REUNION WITH SELF

Separation is a big part of the earthly "dream," what Hindus and Buddhists call *maya*. As we continue to traverse the path to unity consciousness, let's look a little closer at this phenomenon we call duality.

Another consequence of the dualistic perspective is what has been called 'willful blindness.' (see Margaret Heffernan's book of the same name (New York: Walker Publishing Co., 2011) We tend not to see what we do not want to see. We tend to be attracted to people who are similar to us, people with similar values, beliefs and attitudes, and to be fearful of those who are not. This is the origin of racism, sexism, classism—you name it. The "Other" is to be feared and/or ostracized. There is a wonderful, must-see PBS documentary called *People Like Us* that deals with this issue of social class in America. When we only accept people like ourselves, it narrows our perspective of life to a small bandwidth. The ego fears that which is different from itself. The first goal of the ego is *prediction and control*. We, in the egoic consciousness, want to feel safe in our separated state (which, of course, is impossible); this is the cause of the great insecurity and anxiety that has been rampant in our world. If someone or something can be predicted and/or controlled, we can seem to get a semblance of security. We become willfully blind when we know we should behave or act in a certain way but we don't do it. When something appears on the screen of our reality, we tend to ignore it if addressing it might shake up our sense of security or safety. We do this even though, at some level, we know this can compromise us and we'll have to clean it up later (think of the Catholic Church ignoring its abusive priests). I know we have all had these experiences. Margaret Heffernan suggests in her book several ways we can deal with this while still in duality: challenging our biases, encouraging debate, discouraging conformity, and not backing away from difficult or complicated problems.

Still another consequence of the dualistic perspective is a related phenomenon, obedience to authority. Stanley Milgram, with his now-famous Milgram experiments, proved this years ago. If a person is told to harm a subject for some reason by what is perceived to be a legitimate authority figure, they will tend to do it; in his experiments, Milgram showed that over 70 percent of the subjects (of all races, sexes, ages, etc.) would willfully harm another human if told to do so by an authority figure. Why is this so? Because, in our separated ego state, we long for someone else to be responsible for our choices so we can have someone to blame if it goes wrong! If you realize that there is only *one being* operating in life, then you recognize there is literally no one to blame! By adopting the position of 100 percent personal responsibility (no blame, no judgment, no criticism), you can find yourself moving into the non-dual state automatically.

I had a good friend who, many years ago, understood how we are all conditioned to obey authority figures. One day, he and I were to play tennis at the University of Houston tennis courts. When we got there, the courts were all full. So my friend, a bit of a psychopath himself, grabbed a clipboard from a bench, walked up to the couple who were playing on court one, and announced that he was in charge of an inter-mural tournament and this court was needed for a match. The couple, without asking for his credentials, obediently walked off the court and we began playing! On one level, this is humorous, but at another level it shows us how deeply conditioned we are to see ourselves as separate from everyone and everything else and to see that some folks are author-ity figures and need to be respected and/or obeyed.

AN ENNEAGRAM PERSPECTIVE ON DUALITY

All of the Enneagram types experience a world of duality. But I would say that the type *most* susceptible to blame (seeing the problem as being out there) is the Type Eight, the Boss. This type glories in its power and loves to have power over others. This was reinforced by a childhood where they saw other people (read: parents and other adults) as not knowing what to do, so they took it into their own hands to decide what the rules for life are. So the Eight comes in with the type in their DNA and it is reinforced with social conditioning.

Eights are take-charge people. They look totally uninhibited but are covering a basic innocence with bravado. They are hard on others, driv-ing them and demanding more from them. But, as hard as they push others, they push themselves more. Their punitive super-ego drives and castigates them, goading them on to be stronger and tougher. And, if things go seemingly wrong, they tend to protect their well-guarded inner tenderness with blame for the person out there who "did wrong." They are often openly arrogant, dismissive and disparaging of others as a cover for their protected inner child.

Eights tend to see the world in black-and-white duality. Either you are with me or against me, says the Eight. Eights love to argue or have a good debate. And they love to fight; this energizes them. They are high-energy folks who are typically *not* good listeners. Above all, they want to be in charge, so you will find lots of leaders in organizations that are Type Eight. If the Eight senses that the current leader in a situation is weak, indecisive or off course, the Eight will take them out and step into the role themselves. But, interestingly, if the current leader is doing a good job (according to the Eight), the Eight will gladly step back and support their efforts.

TRANSCENDING DUALITY AND MOVING INTO THE NEW WORLD

I feel that, once we begin to intuit what is happening to us, around us and through each of us, the people of this planet will begin to let go of their fears and allow the ego to shrink into the background. What can we do collectively to help this process along?

I urge us to come together in groups for meditation or for collective intention. When we come together, we continue to allow for the strengthening of the awakening process for ourselves and all life on the planet. Also, we can help folks who are still deeply trapped and troubled by the duality illusion. It *does* look like the world is going to Hell in a hand-basket, to quote an old phrase.

However, we are, in fact, a creative species, we humans, and with flexibility of mind and heart. We can adjust to these new perceptions we are having. At this moment in time, it appears that we are in the height of the duality phase of human consciousness. Things look pretty bleak.

Yet, as I mentioned earlier, there are signs of awakening consciousness everywhere. Yes, it looks like there is difference everywhere; how can we possibly be One Being? People seem to be locked into separate identities, each needing to validate its perspective and/or denigrate others' perspectives. But imagine what life would be like if we could just let go of this egoic addiction. What if we could feel our Oneness with all life? What if we could live the words of John Lennon's famous song, *Imagine?* I believe it is actually a small step from the seeming paralysis of the waking egoic state to the wonder and glory of the awakened state.

Right now, the planet seems gripped in a state of madness. It seems upside down. But healing is happening. And one way it is being healed is by healing the shadow. Practice patience, compassion and empathy for others seemingly different from you. Know that you are connected to everything else in the cosmos even if it doesn't feel that way ("fake it till you make it"). This is the way out of duality...and into the truth of who and what you really are.

CHAPTER 3

♡

Healing the Shadow

"The evils of the world that confront me are a reflection of my own internal state, and no one can protect me from my own mind."
—Marianne Williamson, May 2, *Course in Miracles* calendar

"The process of personal growth isn't always easy. We must face our own ugliness. We often must become painfully aware of the unworkability of a pattern before we are willing to give it up. It often seems, in fact, that our lives get worse rather than better when we begin to work deeply on ourselves."
—Marianne Williamson, *A Return to Love*

The December 2012 events in Newtown, Connecticut, where 20 kindergarten students and 6 adults were mercilessly gunned down in a shooting at Sandy Hook Elementary School, is perhaps a good example of the unhealed shadow in action. Of course, it could be a result of severe mental illness, but mental illness can be a result of extreme repressed shadow material. In any event, it is instructive to examine this event from a higher perspective. At one level, it is a tragedy: needless death is inflicted by a tortured soul.

However, the outpouring of help and compassion that such an event inspires also brings us closer to unity consciousness. Hurricane Sandy did, and is continuing to do, the same thing. The more people realized that we are "all in this together," the weaker the individualistic ethic will become. So the Newtown event illustrates both the danger inherent in unhealed shadow elements playing out in society, and the gift of caring and compassion that spontaneously emerges with such an event. Now, all that remains is for this caring and compassion to be more than a transient event. And this can only be done by an awakening to Oneness by regular folks.

HOW THE SHADOW WORKS

Let us look in detail at the way such an unhealed shadow presents itself. First, the unhealed person sees the world out there as doing it to them. In other words, they are perceiving their life from a victim consciousness. Likely, this is due primarily to a lack of love received from their caregivers, or the conditional love that they did receive. The wounding of such socialization grows and grows. Eventually, the pressure of this unhealed shadow builds and builds, and finally explodes into rage and resentment at something external to themselves. This is what we are seeing all too commonly in the world around us—just look at the daily newspaper. And why do you suppose violence and mayhem sells papers and media so well? Because it appeals to our unhealed subconscious and it allows us to vicariously experience what we ourselves would like to do: attack something outside ourselves in return for the pain we experience in our separated experience of self.

"War is a drug," according to the award-winning film *the Hurt Locker*, directed by Kathryn Bigelow. One of the most poignant parts of the film is the last scene; the demolition expert finally returns from Iraq to his wife and family…and then can't wait to get back into the war zone so he can act the hero and dismantle more explosive devices. What does this statement mean? It means that we are drawn to war as a way to vicariously release the hurt contained in our unhealed shadows. This is also what Eckhart Tolle calls "the pain body" in his best-selling book *The Power of Now*.

Of course, neither war nor any other expression of the unhealed shadow or pain body does anything to dissolve it. It remains in our unconscious, waiting for another opportunity to strike out at those "bad people out there." And almost every person has a pain body, filled with unhealed wounds and hurts from their past, so the collective pain body or shadow is expressed often as war against those so-called enemies out there.

Remember; there are only two ways to perceive life: through love or fear. Anger is an aspect of fear. When we repress our hurts, we set ourselves up for the introduction of anger into our consciousness. Why? Because the place we go to in anger can be thought of as our internal barrier. Any situation that pushes our buttons is a situation where we don't yet have the capacity to be unconditionally loving. That is the bottom line.

And, as Marianne Williamson points out, the purpose of life is to grow into our perfection. As the Bible says, we are made in the image and likeness of God. We just have to remove the barriers to that unconditional love. Another way to say this is that we are already enlightened; we just have to remove the barriers to that experience. Once we awaken to the reality of our Oneness with all life, shadow elements will have no power over us. Or, stated differently, the shadow might still be there but its ability to dictate our perception will be weakened or completely removed. The shadow cannot survive the power of unconditional love.

As was mentioned earlier, the shadow is nothing but parts of our own personalities that have been repressed into our subconscious because they were unacceptable to some others—usually, to our caregivers. Since our behavior was unacceptable and we depended so strongly on the love (conditional love) of our caregivers, we had to repress these aspects for our survival...or so we thought. The shadow is our hurt stored up for years (maybe even past lives?) that acts to distort our perceptions of the outer world. If you were raised in a brutal household, whether physically brutal or emotionally brutal or both, you will experience a world full of danger and possible brutality. This is why abused children often become abusers themselves.

As a child, I was whipped by my father (6'5" tall and over 200 pounds) with his belt as punishment for so-called wrongdoing. I learned many years later that when he was a child, his father would come home every day from work and whip him and his four brothers for what they had done wrong that day. As I began to do shadow work, I discovered that one reason I acted out in my childhood was that it got my father's attention. My dad was an introverted Five on the Enneagram, completely shut off from his feelings. So if I could get him to whip me, at least he was paying attention to me.

This is a basic psychological principle: people would rather have negative attention than be ignored. When I became a father, I would whip my sons when they had done wrong, too, following the same pattern—until one day, while I was whipping my son, I flashed on my father whipping me....and vowed in that moment to stop whipping them. But later, with my young daughter, I whipped her a few times...until one day, in the front seat of the car in Sacramento, I felt how wrong it was and I told her "I am never going to whip you again." The look of relief on her face said it all. That was the last whipping for any of my children.

Once repressed, shadow elements show up externally to us as qualities in others that we don't like, or as events and circumstances that represent that aspect that is unhealed in us. In my case, part of my shadow was punishing so-called wrong behavior outside myself. These shadow aspects become crystallized in us as beliefs, attitudes and /or values that represent the unhealed shadow. The sequence of events looks something like this: (1) violence, neglect and/or conditional love from caregivers gives the child instructions on how to be in the world to get love; (2) this socialization process works well in shaping the child's behavior; (3) this sets up the duality of good and bad behavior; (4) the child represses the bad as unacceptable; and (5) voila! We have the shadow.

Everything that Spirit (Source, God) created was and is the language of love. Even in this world of shadows, love reveals the intent and nature of life's design. These outer forms are intended to reveal the universal I AM—love. The language of love is currently bastardized by false spiritual and emotional loves in human beings, where love of this and that have superseded the love for Source, God, Spirit. Remember the First Commandment? "Thou shalt love the Lord thy God with all thy heart, and with all thy soul, and with all thy mind." (Matthew 22:37) He wasn't kidding! And He didn't mean love for a concept, a mental image, of God. He meant love for the character of God, namely, compassion, forgiveness, kindness, openness, and so forth.

The Earth and all its living forms are designed to respond to this language of love. All of creation actually understands this language. You could call this the Tone of Being. As we convey this Tone with our words, actions, gestures, and so on, we convey this creative spirit into this dark world of shadows. We love to give and receive love in some way—to touch or be touched. This process operates at all levels. For example, in the levels of consciousness, we love to think about someone or something with love, and we like to be thought of with love.

Even in this shadowy world, don't we see how amazing life is? And yet our *perception* of reality is only a shadow of the vaster adventure of reality. Until we can actually experience reality as it is, let us be thankful for what we do know and experience!

AN ENNEAGRAM PERSPECTIVE ON THE SHADOW

All nine types have shadow elements, but the Type Four seems to suffer the most with its shadow. Type Four is the Tragic Romantic, and they seem to suffer more than the other types. This arises from an inner hopelessness about ever being truly content. Fours are envious of others who seem to have it all together while the Fours themselves most certainly do not. Sometimes Four's try to present themselves as buoyant and optimistic, but this merely belies the despair behind the façade. They tend to be socially insecure, afraid of not being loved or included. They tend to feel alone, abandoned and estranged from others.

The Type Four is melancholic, and this is because, in early childhood, they experience themselves as being disconnected from Being. After that experience of abandonment, they live their lives with a kind of angst and an inner sense of despair. "Something important is missing" is the inner cry of the Four. The inner experience of the Four is that of being a separate someone who is cut off from Being and is set adrift. This is the core of their shadow experience.

HOW TO WORK WITH THE SHADOW

A good way to work with the shadow is to say to yourself: "Since it looks like the problem is over there in some other person or situation, and I know there is a unity to life, then I must be projecting it out there." This is the magician trick of the ego. It really looks like the problem is out there...but it isn't. Everything that I experience is contained with me.

With any upset that looks like it is caused out there, a good practice is to slow down, get quiet and ask: "What does this situation or person have to teach me?" This is where ruthless honesty (or what Tara Brach calls *radical acceptance*) comes in. We have to be willing to feel the unacceptable parts of ourselves for them to heal. We need to feel it all the way through, until the charge on it dissipates.

Often, this is easier said than done. Journaling can be helpful for this. Write down your experience of being triggered or activated emotionally by another person and get quiet inside. Ask yourself, "What is this telling me?" If you are willing to be honest, the answer will come. This inner work is a very powerful way to dissolve these unacceptable parts and integrate them into the wholeness of your being, thereby releasing lots of creative energy that had been tied up in the egoic dream (or delusion) of separation. Many people report increased energy and wakefulness when shadow elements are successfully integrated into their consciousness.

Another useful modality is conscious breathing. When you feel yourself hooked by the urge to blame another for your situation, or perhaps to act out the pain of your particular Enneagram fixation, just move your conscious awareness into your belly and do some slow, deep breathing. This will calm your mind down and allow for the so-called problem to dissipate. Reaction comes from mental and/or emotional upset, not from the body. By breathing into the belly, we short-circuit the reaction until we get back in charge.

Of course, if you wait too long, the fixation (an Enneagram term for the rigid fixed view of yourself when you feel you have to be a certain way) will take hold and seem to become you; at this point, you will likely not be able to notice how you have lost your awareness of yourself as part of one being. You have now become a small self, full of fear or resentment or whatever.

If this happens, forgive yourself. You will have other chances to continue the healing process. To paraphrase Rumi, the Sufi poet: when you make a mistake and fall down, get up yet again and again. Until the shadow is completely integrated, you will have reactions to other people and circumstances. When little or no reaction occurs, that is how you will know that you are living in an awakened state!

A final modality I have used is to feel the pain of the reaction all the way though. One of my Enneagram mentors (Eli Jaxon-Bear) calls it allowing the pain to burn all the way through. The natural reaction is to run away from pain, so this practice is counter-intuitive. However, it is one of the quickest and most effective ways to clear out the shadow. Of course, actually feeling the pain is the last thing you want to do! But if you want to be free of the shadow and its power over your thoughts, feelings and behavior, such a practice can be very useful.

WHEN THE SHADOW IS HEALED

How will you know when you have healed your shadow? When you can welcome everything with little or no reactions! When you can recognize, understand, moderate and work with your reactions, you are well on your way. When you can welcome and accept everything that comes to you at the deepest level, you will be in union with everything...which is your goal.

Another thing you will notice is your unconditional love for everyone and everything. In other words, duality will be healed at the same time. Judgment and resistance will be gone or lessened to a major degree. You will be able to see everything as an extension of yourself. Therefore, there is no need to compare yourself with another, or react to anyone or any situation, for that matter. Wonder and joy will be your constant companion as you experience the various aspects of yourself with thankfulness and forgiveness.

Obviously, there is a transition period involved here. Many souls are not willing to heal their shadow selves, primarily due to fear. They will, for a while, continue to play the blame game, looking outside themselves for the cause of their misery. Therefore, we will continue to see elements of the unhealed shadows of others (and ourselves, if we are not willing to do this work). Don't worry; this is to be expected. All you have to do is your part, which is to heal your shadow. After all, you still look like an individual "I" (the small egoic self). Since all is actually one in reality, healing your shadow will play a role in healing the collective shadow. And remember, as you rise in vibration and consciousness, your rise will assist the whole of consciousness to rise up out of the denser three-dimensional world of time and space in which you and I have been living.

We are beginning to enter a Golden Age that has been prophesized for millennia. As the collective shadow heals, we will begin to see and experience a new world, one in which pain, misery, despair and resentment have all but disappeared. Give thanks; a new day is dawning!

CHAPTER 4

♡

The Role of Gratitude

"We find our happiness to the extent to which we use our minds to bless the world, for that is the natural use of the mind. It is the reason we were born."
—Marianne Williamson, *Illuminata: A Return to Prayer*

A dear friend of mine said many years ago, "Cultivate an attitude of gratitude." Why is this so important? Because gratitude sends out an electromagnetic pulsation that allows you to receive love. Many people wait for another to be loving towards them before they can trust that person and then extend love to them. This is backwards. You must extend love first, and this creates a pathway for love to flow to you. This sends out a frequency that allows for manifestation that is based on love.

Remember, there are only two basic emotions: fear and love. Think of it this way: love expands, fear contracts. It is not that fear is "bad" and love is "good." Those polarities are part of our dualistic perspective. It is just that using love as the manifesting current, so to speak, allows for love-based experiences and circumstances to manifest. Said differently, you are manifesting on a current of love, rather than a current of fear.

The world now seems gripped by fear. And, of course, it has been shown that encouraging fear enables the few to control the many:

In a conversation in his cell in 1946, the Nazi Goering said this:

Naturally, the common people don't want war.... But after all, it is the *leaders* of a country who determine the policy and it is always a simple matter to drag the people along, whether it is a democracy or a fascist dictatorship or a Parliament or a communist dictatorship.... The people can always be brought to the bidding of the leaders. That is easy. All you have to do is to tell them they are being attacked and denounce the pacifists for lack of patriotism and exposing the country to danger. It works the same in every country.

The attacks of 9/11 and other so-called terrorist events keep us locked into this contractive energy. And if people are afraid, they are easy to control. Right now, the debate in the national media is the so-called choice between liberty and safety. It has been shown over and over that people will choose authoritarian control over anarchy. If we are afraid, we want someone to rescue us and give us leadership that will tell us what to do to feel safe. This is why the so-called police state is so prevalent in the world now. This is the culmination of the dualistic state, out of which we are now moving.

Unwilling to take personal responsibility for the reality they themselves have created, people in dualism look outside themselves for a "savior." Too often this savior has been an authoritarian control freak (i.e., Adolf Hitler, Benito Mussolini, Saddam Hussein, Fidel Castro, etc.)! But the reason fear *can* grip us is that we are identified with the small egoic self, which thinks it is the body—and bodies can be hurt or killed. If one were truly in the Higher Self identity, which is infinite and eternal, then fear could have *no* foothold at all!

THE WAY OUT OF FEAR

The way out of the fear state is gratitude. When we are thankful, we allow our hearts to open and we feel the connection with the *one heart*. Remember, we are all *one being* in truth, despite appearances. When we are thankful for our lives, we send the signal that all of what shows up in our personal realities is really good. Even if it appears to be bad from the dualistic perspective, whatever shows up is exactly what you drew to yourself to be loved and/or integrated. This, again, is another way the shadow is integrated. And, if we want to increase the power of love on the planet, then the best way to do this is to be thankful in all things. This is essentially saying that we need to love whatever shows up in our lives.

But if we increase the power of fear by being judgmental, critical and blaming of others (or toward ourselves), we increase the contractive force on the whole and we reinforce the belief that we are separate from the so-called outside world. Fortunately, love vibrates at a much higher frequency than fear. So a few people vibrating at a much higher frequency than the many can cancel out the deleterious effects of the fear pattern, as David Hawkins (*Power vs. Force*) has told us.

And, from an individual perspective, let us not forget the words of the Bible: "For the thing which I greatly feared is come upon me, and that which I was afraid of is come unto me." (Job 3:25) When my wife and I lived in Rogers Park on the north side of Chicago, our landlady, a small and very fearful lady, had a Doberman who walked with her, and she also had six locks on her door! She had been robbed several times, which, of course, provided the self-fulfilling prophecy that the world is to be feared. In other words, vibrating at the low frequency of fear will cause you to draw things that are fearful to yourself. I realize that this sounds like I am blaming the victim, but lower fear vibrations do attract the things that are feared. Now, I realize that people do have experiences that aren't caused by them being fearful, but the point I am making is this: if you fear something enough, that which you fear is drawn towards you.

THE VICTIM EXPERIENCE AND GRATITUDE

By this, I don't mean you need to blame yourself for drawing so-called bad things to yourself. You are not a victim of your life experience. It simply means that I am the creator of my world. By taking 100 percent responsibility for my creations, I move out of the victim state and become a conscious creator. The truth is we are creating all the time, but most of our creations are done unconsciously...through our beliefs, attitudes and values. I remember a great quote from the est training back in the 1970s: "If you want to know what you intended to have, look at what you got!"

Here is another example from my life, this time one of love being the manifesting current. Years ago, I was in a home outside of Paris, France, and an elderly woman showed up. I found out she was the Peace Pilgrim; maybe you have heard of her? She told this story. As you may know, the Peace Pilgrim traveled all over spreading the message of peace. Hitchhiking along the way, she trusted that the right people would show up and provide what she needed on any day. One day, a man picked her up, and instantly she sensed that he wanted to hurt her. So she said to him, "Thank you for picking me up. I can tell that you are a nice man and are interested only in my safety and health. I am tired so I am going to sleep a while. I am so thankful you picked me up." And she went to sleep. This completely disarmed the world-be rapist and, for the next few years, he traveled with her as a guard so she would be safe.

THE ENNEAGRAM PERSPECTIVE ON GRATITUDE

Of course, all the Enneagram types can be grateful, but it probably comes easiest to the Type Seven, the Epicure. Sevens are naturally buoyant and optimistic and they tend to give everything a positive spin. They view the world with rose-colored glasses. Of course, this tends to mask their buried inner pain. They move from *wanting* to be joyful to *having* to be joyful. So the Seven is naturally grateful for almost everything but this can often be derived from their shadow.

Anger, aggression, emptiness and fear are not OK for a Seven to feel or express. They can use their natural charm to defuse another's aggression. They must constantly distract themselves from their negative feelings. However, as the Type Seven grows in their awareness and maturity, they become naturally grateful for their lives. I know this to be true from my personal experience since I am a Type Seven myself. I feel a gratitude for my life almost constantly and this is certainly not something I am trying to do. It is very natural to me.

PLATO'S CAVE METAPHOR

Can you see that any manifestation of fear is simply a reinforcement of the separated state that is egoic consciousness, and that gratitude brings a sense of Oneness? The dualistic state automatically produces the illusion that we call reality.

This reminds me of the philosopher Plato who gave us the "Allegory of the Cave." It goes like this: People in the dualistic state are facing a blank wall in a cave. They are yoked in such a way that they cannot turn their heads. Behind them is a fire, and between the fire and them are various forms whose shadows are projected on the wall. In time, people began to think of the shadows as reality. Plato suggested that if one of them were released and introduced to the wondrous world outside the cave, and then came back and told the others that their cave isn't the real world, he would be laughed at and not believed. If he kept it up, he would be killed for his "heresy."

Plato was trying to say that, in reality, there is a far more wonderful world at another level than is currently being experienced. This world is the world created by an experience of Oneness with all life. We, living now in this world of duality, have sensed the presence and immediacy of this higher realm.

Plato also spoke of love. He wasn't talking about sexual love, although I am sure that was not excluded. He talked about *ideal love,* which he said was a natural state of Oneness and affinity for all sentient life forms. How beautiful! He also said that the greatest friendships pointed in the direction of the Divine, always encouraging a contemplation and study of this realm.

Shadows as now experienced are cast by distortions in human consciousness and then projected out into the realm of outer forms. The shadow is then a distorted mental and/or emotional projection of pain that has not been brought into the light to be integrated. Until we are willing to do our own personal work of integrating our shadow elements, we must not be surprised to see so-called bad things continue to happen in the outer world of form. As mentioned in the previous chapter, the recent mass shootings at Newtown, Connecticut, are such an example.

THE IDEAL LEVEL OF BEING

Jesus himself pointed to this ideal level of Being when He said: "He that hath seen me hath seen the Father" (John 14:9), and "Be ye therefore perfect, even as your Father which is in heaven is perfect" (Matthew 5:48). What did he mean by this? What these quotes are saying is that we are inherently perfect and whole. And isn't it true that, although we still see the shadow elements in ourselves and in others, we are beginning to also see the Divine within them and us? He went on to say: "Let your light so shine before men, that they may see your good works, and glorify your Father which is in Heaven." (Matthew 5:16) This does not mean to do good works so the ego self can be stroked. It means do good works because all is *one*, and when you help another, you are actually helping yourself!

So, as I said before, everything that God or Life created was and is the language of *love*. People have forgotten how to speak the language of love, because they tend to love money, power, and other things rather than loving the Divine. I do not mean the worship of a concept of God here; this has been done for millennia by well-intentioned people. Has this made the world less fearful? No, to speak the language of love means to express in one's living experience the character of love, of God, of Being. Thankfulness is a natural byproduct of such an outward expression.

This is what could be called spiritual expression. If we express the character of God (or if we act as if we were God—which we inherently are, at our origin), we lessen the impact of dualistic thinking and increase our appreciation of all that is. Remember, judgments of good or bad are simply misperceptions created in the mind-dominated fear state.

ONENESS AS REALITY

In the world now, there is a very organic movement towards Oneness and it is called globalization. Of course, in the grip of dualistic thinking, this is being used to centralize power in the few (the so-called 1 percent). Part of this process is an intensifying urge to communicate, and all the electronic devices are an attempt to facilitate this. But if we use these devices to express the current of love, gratitude and appreciation, then we are doing our part to intensify the experience of Oneness on the planet. On the other hand, by agreeing with the separate-self perceptions, we strengthen that view.

You may have noticed that there is *one power* moving everything. The question is, have you noticed that it is moving you, too? Being trapped in the egoic delusion, you think that you (the egoic, small self) are making things happen. But in this state, everything you try to do misses the mark and produces chaos because it is not connected to the One Power that is moving everything! We must get our outer consciousness to trust this process and let this power move us, too.

The Body of Life is *one*. There is One Power moving every part of the cosmos consciously and simultaneously. This includes our personal worlds. The egoic human mind is almost totally unconscious of this fact, but it can become conscious of it. Our starting point is to express appreciation and thankfulness for everything in our worlds, the so-called good and the so-called bad alike. When we do this in the midst of all the bits and pieces of the world around us that are being moved by the One Power, we can become a conscious focus of love in the part of the world we find ourselves in.

"I love you" is the universal communication of the so-called heavenly state, the higher vibration of *love*. Every atom in existence has a design and purpose in the unfolding of the *one purpose* of life. Life obviously knows exactly what it is doing. When you plant an acorn, it always grows an oak tree, never a mimosa. There is a consistency in life's design that we can count upon.

When we disagree with what shows up in our world, we are strengthening our egoic illusion. But when we welcome in everything, the good and the bad, we weaken our dualistic perspective and build our muscles of unity!

We understand that there is interference in parts of the human world, caused primarily by unhealed shadow and by wanting things to be the way we want them to be. However, we are still part of this overall *one* design of life. The One Power is coordinating everything all the time. Very often, our situations and experiences could cause us to doubt this fact. Some things do not feel the way we would like them to feel. But, regardless, they feel the way they feel. Resisting this fact just builds up the egoic delusion. By being thankful for things, we can recognize that everything is in process and our human minds, in duality, cannot accurately judge whether something is actually good or bad.

A CAVEAT

There is one type of human being that seemingly cannot access their hearts. These are the so-called psychopaths or sociopaths. These people are manipulative, superficial, obsessed with materialism, show no empathy or compassion but can fake it... These folks are actually dangerous. They probably have huge, buried shadow material in their consciousness and the pain of that leads them to identify totally with their damaged egos, caring nothing for others. Granted, their condition may also be due to other factors, such as a significant chemical imbalance.

I am not sure that these folks can be healed by any therapy we now know, so, from my perspective, let us not be naïve. Don't expect these people to behave as any normal person would behave. This does not mean that they are unworthy of love; just the contrary. But, as we love them, we also must be aware that they do not flow with the same moral compass of everyone else. So, "Be ye therefore wise as serpents, and harmless as doves" (Matthew 10:16).

GRATITUDE AND THE CURRENT OF LIFE

So, realizing that our immediate circumstance is part of this larger coordinated picture (you could call it the Divine Design in action), difficult though it may be at times, we should try to include everything that is happening in our experience—include it all. We recognize that all is in process and part of the *one movement*, and we trust in this larger process and let it move without our interference or resistance. An analogy perhaps is going down the river in a canoe. The current carries us and we dip our oar in now and then to adjust the direction slightly, and thus we move adroitly in this vast yet immediate process.

The way to fully enjoy the adventure of life is to let go to this larger rhythm or flow. If we express the true character of Being through being thankful, among other things, we are operating optimally in every situation. Earlier I noted that Jesus said, "Be ye therefore perfect." Humans have thought that this meant to live up to some imagined divine ideal. But the true meaning of that word *perfect* is to do exactly what is required in the situation in which we find ourselves, as best we may, given our flawed human equipment of minds and hearts. If we do this, we are expressing the quality of character that is our highest. That is what we must do to escape the gravitational field of the ego and its picture of duality.

So, when we move with the current of life moving in the moment, we play our part in the overall outworking of the one purpose, and we thereby know fulfillment. We can be increasingly confident that we have a part to play in the body of mankind as the evolving Universe unfolds. If we give our finest in every moment, that is perfection. So, remembering this fact and being thankful for all things, we move in harmony with the larger cycles of creation that are unfolding in every moment and we know the peace of the non-dual state. Sure, things are intensifying in the world, and it will become even more intense. But if we hold our focus of thankfulness, we will know how to move in the midst of this increasing pressure.

Gratitude is a very important step in spiritual maturity and to true success in life. It helps focus the attention away from the demands of the ego and places it outside our selfish desires. Some people put a stone or gem in their pocket to remind them to be thankful. Several times a day, you can rub the stone and remember all the things you can be thankful for...including those you didn't want! It also serves to keep a positive vibration flowing in your consciousness. Gratitude in case of illness can sometimes reverse the condition; remember, the body is an artifact of the mind. Gratitude is the antidote for the "poor me," victim consciousness. And it is a manifestation of your love for everything in your world.

CHAPTER 5

♡

The Role of Service

*"One key to abundance in every area of life is this: We experience
God's peace and harmony to the extent to which we love, forgive,
and focus on the good in others and in ourselves....*
*"In time we give, in devotion we show, in efforts to love and serve
and forgive each other, we partake of the spiritual connection that
restores the link between the Father and His separated children."*
—Marianne Williamson, *Illuminata*

*"There is only one of us here. What we give to others, we give to ourselves.
What we withhold from others, we withhold from ourselves. In any moment,
when we choose fear over love, we deny ourselves the experience of Paradise."*
—Marianne Williamson, *A Return to Love*

What is serving others, anyway? If it is coming from an attitude of
"I feel sorry for you and want to help you," is this genuine service? If helping comes from this attitude, it is hierarchical in nature; it is,
in effect, saying that I have more than you and I will stoop down to help
you. This is *not* genuine helping.

I prefer to call genuine helping *sharing*; in other words, I can share
what I have with you without any taint of demeaning you and looking
down on you. I have a good friend who uses this acronym when she feels

stressed: DSFSQ. It stands for "Do Something For Someone Quick!" If our focus is too self-centered, we find ourselves stressed out and tense; helping another is a very fast way to feel better. So, in a very real sense, service *is* self-centered because it makes you feel good. And a corollary to this is that, when we focus exclusively on ourselves and our problems, we feel worse, don't we? Suffering ensues.

Consider the words of His Holiness the Dalai Lama, in his recent book *Ethics for a New Millennium*: "A proper appreciation of the workings of cause and effect suggests that far from being powerless, there is much we can do to influence our experience of suffering." Old age, sickness and death are inevitable. But, "as with torrents of negative thoughts and emotions, we certainly have a choice in how we respond to our experience of suffering. If we wish, we can adopt a more dispassionate and rational approach, and on that basis we can discipline our response to it." On the other hand, we can simply fret about our misfortunes, but when we do, we become frustrated. As a result, "afflictive emotions arise and our peace of mind is destroyed. When we do not restrain our tendency to react negatively to suffering, it becomes a source of negative thoughts and emotions. There is thus a clear relationship between the impact suffering has on our heart and mind and our practice of inner discipline."

An important question related to service might be: If we truly are all *one being*, who are you helping anyway? Of course, in our separated egoic identity, there seem to be others outside of us whom we might help or ignore. But the truth is that we are all one being. So if we are helping another, we are literally helping ourselves, even if it doesn't look that way. In our current state of amnesia (or the collective dream of separation), it appears that helping another takes something from us. But anyone who has really given selflessly knows that the psychic rewards for doing so are great. Why is this? Because at some level we know that helping others is really helping ourselves.

The term *Self* also overcomes the dualistic notion that one is separated from God. Historically, the picture that there is a sinner down here on Earth and there is a God up there somewhere in heaven is the viewpoint of the ego. Thus, to most people, the term *God* implies otherness. However, there is no separation in the Allness of Creation, so it is impossible for the created to be separate from the Creator. Enlightenment is therefore the revelation of the Self when the illusion of the reality of a separate self is removed.

David Hawkins speaks of this in his book *I: Reality and Subjectivity*: "The constant awareness of one's existence as 'I' can be the ever present expression of the innate divinity of the Self"—that is, unless we're referring to the egoic "I". "This is a universal, constant experience that is purely subjective and of which no proof is possible or necessary. The 'I' of the Self is the expression of Divinity as Awareness, which is therefore beyond time and form."

This appears to be a bit of a paradox. The "I" that is the separated self is the ego; however, you can use the term to indicate the transcendental or divine "I." Hawkins continues: "The truth of this identity is obscured by the duality created by perception and disappears when all points of view are relinquished."

THE DIFFERENCE BETWEEN SERVICE AND ENABLING

When you enter the realm of service, you are quickly confronted with the issue of enabling. Enabling refers to the help which keeps another person from taking personal responsibility for their life. Why do we do these kinds of helping? We might feel sorry for the person, we might have an unconscious urge to hinder their progress, we might be jealous, or have other reasons. Alcoholics Anonymous uses this term a lot. If help is not actually helpful in inviting a person to a higher level of independent function, then one must ask the question: Is this help actually helping the person or maintaining them in a state of victim consciousness?

The only kind of service that we can be quite sure will be helpful is that which is aligned with Divine Purpose. How can we know this? By getting quiet inside and asking the question: What would be of the highest good for this person in this situation right now? If what we wish to do is so aligned, then, by all means, do the act of service. The enabler, of course, will do this and conclude that they need to rescue the person one more time. Here is where discernment comes in…and ruthless inner honesty.

If our service is really a sacred act of service to life itself, then there will be no hesitation. One is compelled to help by a spiritual impulse. This is because we sense our connectedness with all life. Therefore, there is no separation between helping another and helping all of life. But if we stay locked into the separated self, it will seem like one must take care of number one, as the saying goes.

There is a wonderful expression, again from Alcoholics Anonymous: "Fake it until you make it." This means that we can pretend to be part of a unified whole, even if our perceptual apparatus tells us that we are separate from all life. The more we act in this pretend mode, the closer we come to the realization that we are no longer pretending!

A side note here on Alcoholics Anonymous might be useful. One of the strengths of AA comes from the fellowship, the realization that there is a natural unity or connection among addicts. This is a kind of oneness-awakening, albeit at a microcosmic level. When humans see themselves as part of a larger family of people, they can see the oneness in that group. The rub comes when they see others outside that select group as separate from them; then the problems arise.

Another important consideration is this: In the egoic world that I have already said is illusory, who exactly are we helping? In our almost exclusive focus outside ourselves in the so-called outer world, no less a philosopher than Plotinus (a neo-Platonist) argues that this singular focus clouds the mirror inward to the soul. If we cannot see into ourselves, then what we see outside is clouded by the afore-mentioned shadow elements present in our psyche (this is called projection). Another way of putting this is to say that our inner mirror—our consciousness—has become foggy and tarnished by our over-concern for material and worldly things.

MEDITATION (SERVING THE TRUE SELF) VS. SERVING ONE'S EGOIC SELF

Consumerism and materialism have served to divert our attention away from the inner worlds...where the real power lies! If service is genuine and selfless, it promotes Oneness. If it is done to get something from another or to aggrandize one's ego, it promotes separation.

The promise of materialism, either explicit or implicit, is that, by buying this product, you will be happy and/or content. But it never works, does it? So we keep trying to draw more things to ourselves, whether in the form of material goods or acclamation and praise from others, in the hope that they will make us happy...which, of course, they never can do except for momentary pleasure. The research on happiness shows clearly that, after a certain base level, more stuff does not make us any happier!

This is where the power of meditation comes in. If we focus our attention inward, we lessen the power of the external world to influence our dualistic tendencies. In deep meditation, we realize that everything is fine; there are no problems. Problems are simply a manifestation of duality; we imagine some things are good and some things are bad.

In the present moment, do you have any problems? In meditation, we come to the still point within which problems cannot exist. Problems are time-bound, meaning that problems can only exist in time. In the present, there are no problems. So if someone seems to need help, we are seeing that part of ourselves that has not been integrated yet into our natural state of wholeness. Who is that person seemingly in need of our help? Well, it is a part of us! If we can extend unconditional love to that seeming person outside of us, we are giving unconditional love to ourselves; what could be a better gift?

SERVICE AS A RESPONSE TO DIVINE PROMPTING

As we learn to listen to that still, small voice inside, we begin to align ourselves with our larger Divine Purpose. In this alignment, we automatically know what to do and how to do it. You actually do not need to plan for the future; if you are awake to each present moment and the opportunities and constraints it offers, you will know what to do. This is a foolproof recipe for peaceful living. Planning is for the fearful ego which is constantly worried about survival. And worry it should, as the ego has no idea what to do in the present moment, since it lives exclusively in the past or the future. Having said that, there is no danger in planning as long as it is a flexible plan, subject to change as the spiritual prompting indicates.

If you are in the present moment, alert to the divine promptings, you will know how to serve. And you will know who to serve, also. This is not enabling. Spirit knows exactly what is needed in every situation. Trusting spirit to guide you is the smartest thing you can do. And this type of service could be called sacred service. Sacred service is what you do when you feel the prompting of Spirit. If you do something for another because you want praise, thanks, recognition, or to feel good about yourself, this is all egoic service.

THE ENNEAGRAM PERSPECTIVE ON SERVICE

All types can be service-oriented, but the type who naturally gravitates towards service is the Type Two, the Giver or the Helper. Ingratiating themselves with others, Twos try to make themselves indispensable. Their need for love and approval is extreme—they feel dependent on it—and they try to win love by *pleasing* the object of their affection. So they give freely, pretending they have no needs of their own, and they do it to get love. This is not unconditional love. In fact, it is very conditional and the Two, after giving and giving in service to others, can get to the point of anger if they aren't sufficiently appreciated and/or recognized.

Twos want to be seen as loving, generous, kind, empathetic and, above all, always there for others. They deny their own needs; in fact, they often are not conscious at all of what they need and want. Their image is of being the lovable person, always ready to serve others. They have difficulty saying no to anyone and they are the ultimate co-dependent personality.

SERVICE AS AN ANTIDOTE TO SELF-CENTEREDNESS

Service is one of the best ways to get out of the self-centered trap of the ego. If life is all about me (the imagined separated self), then there is no room for service. Furthermore, there is no incentive to serve, if it is all about me. But by extending myself to serve another, even if it seems like I am helping another separate person, the effect is one of healing. Do yourself a favor and give an act of selfless service. It will make you feel better and it will also allow you to look inward and begin to clear out the shadow elements that are clouding the lens, so to speak, of your soul. What could be better?

Volunteer service can be started with a very self-centered ego. The person doing it wants to enhance their image of themselves as a wonderful, giving person. However, as the service continues, the person can gradually see themselves in the other people and their egoic concern can shift, even if temporarily. Examples of this are volunteers who help in times of tragedy like with Hurricane Katrina, or the typhoon that hit the Philippines. When the focus of attention shifts away from "me" and "my concerns," there can be a wonderful breakthrough to Oneness.

THE VALUE OF SERVICE

Finally, let us summarize the value of service. If we want to discover our identity with the All, our true identity, then our case of mistaken identity with the small, fearful ego must be relinquished. Then the so-called fall from grace, alluded to earlier, can be reversed by realizing that it never really happened. We have been operating in a delusional state, thinking that we are separate from all of life, when in truth we never have been separated from God or each other—we just *thought* we were.

But for most of us, the Fall has to be reversed gradually, step-by-step. There are several ways to reverse it: by healing the shadow, by being thankful for all things, by living a life of selfless service, through meditation to discover our inner reality, by surrender to the Inner Urge or Presence... all of these are important. But, as Swami Ramdas says, "There are two ways [to liberation]: one is to expand your ego to infinity, and the other is to reduce it to nothing—the former by knowledge, and the latter by devotion. The [knowledge holder] says: 'I am God, the Universal Truth.' The devotee says: 'I am nothing, O God, You are everything.' In both cases, the ego-sense disappears."

Use service as a powerful and fruitful personal path to liberation. But be careful that you are not using it to aggrandize your ego about how good you are being. Give without concern for results. That is the key.

CHAPTER 6

♡

The Present Moment

"Crucifixion is the energy pattern of fear, the manifestation
of a closed heart. Resurrection is the reversal of that pattern,
brought about by a shift in thought from fear to love."
—Marianne Williamson, *A Return to Love*

What is the present moment? Part of living in the three-dimensional reality we inhabit is the illusion of time and space. We seem to have a past (things that seem to have happened to us before this moment and are contained in what is called memory) and that which will seemingly happen to us at some later time (future). Yet, when we really examine this thing we call time, we find that the time is always now and that we progress from one moment of now into another in a seamless progression.

It is factually always now; there is no other time that is real. The past and the future are both illusory and are projections of the mind. One way to discover the present moment is this: release all judgments, evaluations, criticisms, and stories you have about the past and let go of all concern and expectations that you might have about the future and voila: you will find yourself in the present moment!

Aha, you say: easier said than done! Yes, this is true; we have well-ingrained habits of thought that take us into the imaginary past and future. This is the ego's work. It does not want you to stay in the present

moment because then it cannot work its magic of making you dissatisfied, bored, angry or whatever. So just take a few minutes and notice how
often your mind pulls you into musing about the past and/or dreaming
about the future. Some Enneagram types do this more than others but
it is a common human habit. And, as I say, the ego is committed to keeping you dissatisfied and wanting what you don't have.

Try this exercise, excerpted from the *Opening Heart Practice* DVD by
Sherry and Thomas White:

- Take a deep, cleansing breath.
- Let go of all that has transpired before this present moment.
- Let go of all concern for what might come in the future.
- Enter the present moment.
- Experience the sacredness that underlies all life.
- Lean back into the compassionate embrace of the Divine.
- Feel the one heart that connects all humanity.
- Open to the wonder of unconditional love.
- Give thanks for it all.

In the present moment, there is a perfect letting go to the inner
urge of the Higher Self, the God-being that is truly you. In this state,
there is a recognition of that which just *is*. No judgment, no critique,
no analysis of good or bad, and one ceases to want anything from the
external world. There is no effort to strive, struggle or climb the ladder
of success. There is only peace. When we're not trying to achieve so-
called good rewards or avoid so-called bad outcomes, we can focus on
responding to the inner urge of Spirit, abiding in a realization of (and
love for) what is.

In the present moment, there is a trusting of the working of what
could be called the Divine Design, the template of each of our lives, and
we yield to that. Then we find that all the wisdom and power we need

are present. We will know what to do in each present moment to come if we just yield to the inner direction. What could be simpler? But, of course, the ego wants none of this! The ego, to survive, wants conflict, rejection of what is, comparison, judgment and non-acceptance.

MEDITATION AND THE PRESENT MOMENT

This is why mediation is so useful. If one can simply let go of all thought, one enters the realm of no-thought, a realm where Being resides and where time disappears. The thinking mind is designed to do one thing only, and that is to be active, thinking about things. Thinking on the surface of the mind will always be illusory because it depends upon the senses for input and the senses are notoriously unreliable. To our senses, the sun appears to rise in the east and set in the west, but science tells us this is not true. There are many optical illusions that you can find on the Internet which again prove the unreliability of the senses.

A reliable way to reach the present moment is through the practice of meditation. Ken Wilber has stated that meditation is the one proven method to raise the level of spiritual development in an individual; in other words, it is guaranteed to raise you up to a higher level of consciousness by its continued use.

Without the anchor of the present moment, life seems without purpose and meaningless. Locked into sense-based perception, the human ego is disconnected from the source of life and tries to be as God—in other words, to act on the basis of their personal will and with desire and/or aversion. The Buddhists tell us that this is a recipe for suffering! There is a wonderful book, written by the sociologist Philip Slater in the 1970s, called *The Pursuit of Loneliness*. In this book, Slater argues that the great loneliness people feel is a spiritual hole or vacuum inside and they vainly try to fill it with consumerism or materialism. Of course, it cannot be filled this way—and this is just fine for businesses that want to sell you something, over and over again! We tell ourselves that if this thing won't fill that void, maybe the next thing will…and on and on we go on the treadmill of life, trying to find fulfillment where it cannot be found.

Life is sacred, but you cannot know this with the mind. I remember a Shamanic training I did years ago. One day I was walking in the woods and suddenly I literally saw the luminous fibers of light that were connecting all trees together in a beautiful web of communion. This alternate reality was not available to my rational, linear mind. Another time, I again was walking in the woods and I stopped to look at a particularly beautiful plant. I had the distinct impression the plant was glad I stopped and noticed it; it said to me that most people just rushed by without ever noticing it at all and it literally appreciated my attention!

These kinds of non-ordinary experiences show us that we are part of the web of life and that nothing is actually separate from anything else. Pretending that we are separate is what causes all the destruction inflicted by humans. Ignoring our connectedness means that we rarely, if ever, do the right thing from the perspective of the One Power moving everything in the cosmos!

THE ENNEAGRAM PERSPECTIVE ON THE PRESENT MOMENT

All Enneagram types tend to live either in the past or the future, but the type that is very susceptible to not being in the present is the Type Six—the Loyal Skeptic. The Six is the core fear type, and Sixes tend to over-prepare for future events to make sure they stay safe. They are trying to achieve prediction and control, so they will lie awake at night before a big event to make sure they are ready for any eventuality. Sixes doubt their perceptions. They question and second-guess everything, are suspicious and lack certainty. Often, they grew up in households where there was alcoholism or mental illness or some other form of instability. The Six learned to get ready for anything.

Both the phobic and the counter-phobic Six are afraid, but the counter-phobic Sixes like to rush into their fear as a way to cope with it. In this way, they superficially look like Eights. Without a recognition of the Essence as the nature of who we are as Beings, the Six substitutes authority figures and rules as their source of certainty. This lack of a true ground creates all sorts of insecurities and fears. Hyper-vigilance is the hallmark of the Six. When Sixes get too stressed out, they become workaholics. When they are centered, they may find the grounding and peacefulness they crave. Many therapists are Sixes; Freud was probably a Six himself.

THE PRESENT MOMENT, THE HEART, AND UNCONDITIONAL LOVE

To live in the present moment, we must access the heart. This is the source of unconditional love. There is a wonderful training offered by the HeartMath folks that helps one access the present moment. If we can make decisions with the heart rather than with the mind (which is not consciously connected with ultimate reality), we will find the source of our intuition and our knowingness. Again, the egoic mind is nothing but a troublemaker when it comes to our lives. The mind, accessing what it calls the past, dredges up guilt and remorse. When it accesses what it calls the future, it can bring up longing, fear and dread. In the present moment, there is not any of that. The present moment is free of all mental constructs; there is no envy, dread, guilt, jealousy, recrimination or fear. There is just now. And, basically, this is all we ever have that is real. Life is, in reality, an unbroken succession of now moments. Future and past are mind-made constructs and definitely lead us into hell.

I was with our nine-month-old granddaughter a few months ago in the UK, driving down the road, and she got really upset that we were keeping her strapped in her car seat. She howled and howled, and finally we got home, got her inside. Almost instantly, she was laughing and giggling, with no trace of her upset. Why did this happen? Because small children are in the present moment! Animals do this too. I saw a couple of ducks one time who were fighting each other; finally, they tired of this game and swam off, unconcerned. Only we humans, with our frontal lobes, can hold resentments, blame, and other negative emotions for a long time. Not such a gift, is it?

GETTING TO THE PRESENT MOMENT

How can we effectively live in the present moment? Practice, practice, practice. And one way to practice is with mindfulness.

Pioneered in the West by the Vietnamese monk Thich Nhat Hanh, mindfulness is a practice which requires single-minded focus on what is happening now. You can do it in the form of a walking meditation, just walking consciously without the stream of the daily 50,000 random thoughts psychologists say we entertain each day. No wonder our minds are tied up in knots! Many of these thoughts are contradictory and/or inconsistent.

For the mind to be a forceful tool for conscious manifestation, it must be single-pointed. Most people allow their mind to wander all over the place, and its power for manifestation is severely limited. Here is where intention comes in: for an intention to produces results, one must hold that intention with no counter-intentions negating it. To do this requires mindfulness.

The more you can stay in the present moment, you more you stay in reality. As I said, the present is all that is real. Everything else is mind-made illusion. Practice staying where it is real! If you are willing to practice this, you will find a rich world will open up to your awareness and you will naturally practice gratefulness. Give it a try!

I had a graphic experience of this fact one morning as I looked out our window in the kitchen and saw the beauty of an early morning sunrise. I was stunned with the beauty of at all. Then my mind jumped in there and said, "Isn't that beautiful?" The picture instantly dulled perceptibly. I was in the present moment but, when I labeled it as beautiful, I called up a memory from the past concerning the beauty of a sunrise. The past is dead, and by mentally labeling my experience, I got out of the present moment!

A final note: The ego hates the present moment. It can only strengthen itself by time-based mind reality—in other words, the past and the future. If we regret the past and/or look forward to the future, we are in the mind and not in the present moment. The ego, as I said before, is interested in resistance to what is. Acceptance and gratitude are anathema to the ego-based identity. So, being thankful for what is, not judging it to be good or bad, surrendering to the inner knowing of your real identity, being alert to the machinations of your shadow (unhealed) elements and being open to ways to serve selflessly are paths to strengthen the presence you are and to weaken the mind-made reality of the ego.

CHAPTER 7

♡

A Return to Oneness

*"Your playing small doesn't serve the world. There's nothing
enlightened about shrinking so that other people won't feel insecure
around you. We are all meant to shine, as children do."*
—Marianne Williamson, *A Return to Love*

We hear the term *oneness* a lot these days; what does it really mean?
It means that all life is connected into a seamless whole. Many
physicists have declared this to be true, including David Bohm and
Fritjof Capra, to name two. Bohm spoke of the "implicate order" in
which the manifest world of forms is contained. Capra, in his classic
book, *The Tao of Physics*, shows us the nature of Oneness as it is demon-
strated in the physical world. Others have called this the Divine Design
or the Divine Template.

But the main point is this: despite appearances, we are connected
to all life. And, perhaps more importantly, life knows exactly what it is
doing in every moment. This is why we can know what to do in every moment if we just yield to this inner wisdom. If we surrender to this knowing and let the egoic identity recede, we find perfect resonance with the
current of life that is animating everything in the cosmos!

There is the "butterfly effect" spoken about by quantum physicists.
The idea is that, when a butterfly flaps its wings, the effects can be felt

around the world. And then there is the work of the radical biologist Rupert Sheldrake, who speaks of "morphogenetic fields." His theory suggests that all species are linked together in a field such that changes in a critical mass of its members automatically produces the same changes in the entire species.

Again, what is Oneness? The reality that we experience in the egoic state sure doesn't look like oneness. It looks like we are in here and everything else is out there, doesn't it? How can Oneness be the reality of the situation?

As I mentioned in Chapter 3, it is a grand magician's trick of the ego. As we begin to individuate, we begin to see our mother as separate from ourselves; then, eventually, everyone else seems to be separate, too. Of course, since the vast majority of humans are caught in this egoic illusion, we get lots of reinforcement for this separatist perspective. The world is effectively run by the human ego, and this produces myriad problems for us. The mind plays this trick on us. The ego is actually a false identity made up by the mind so that we can seem separate from everything outside of us, and thereby be in resistance to whatever appears on the screen of our awareness.

The biggest proof we each have of our separateness is our body. For each of us, our body seems solid and separate from other bodies. If the mind is to be convinced of separateness, then it needs proof, and its proof is the body. The body seems real; it can be hurt, crushed, killed, maimed—what could be more real than that? Our perception is limited by the fact that we live in three-dimensional reality, which operates under certain laws: gravity, cause and effect, and, yes, separateness. So there is literally a consensual agreement that our perception be colored by the assumption of separateness.

Earlier, I spoke of so-called reality as an illusion. There is factually something out there that we perceive with our senses, but what we perceive is not all there is. That is why it called an illusion. There are other dimensions beyond our perceptual apparatus, given our commitment to the separatist doctrine. We literally do not see all there is to reality. Actually, with the five senses, we perceive only a fraction of the multidimensional universe that is available to be seen.

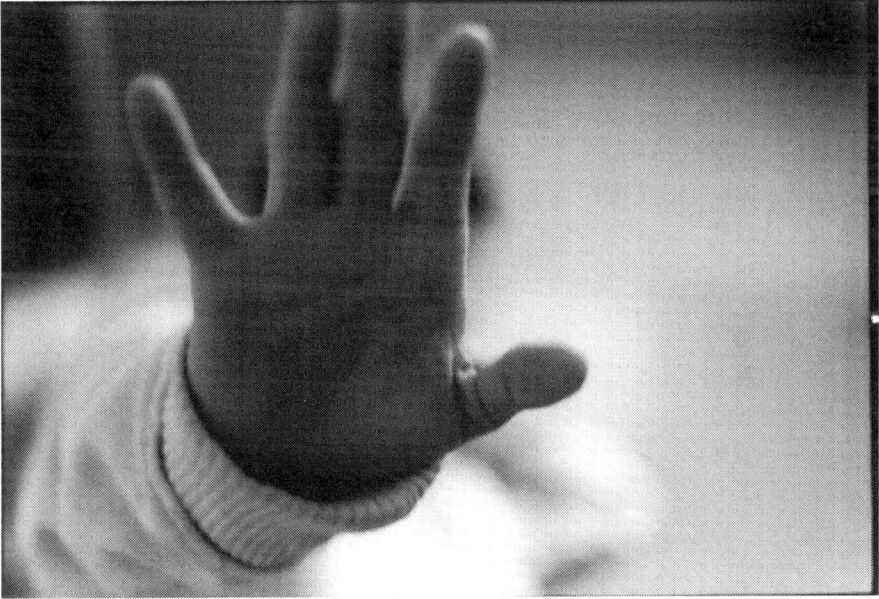

RESISTANCE AND THE EGO

If we resist what is, we strengthen the ego; if we accept (or even love) what is, we weaken it. Remember, the ego is a false identity and, as such, needs to be propped up by our resistance to keep it strong. It has been said that it requires much more energy to keep pretending that everything is separate rather than relaxing into the Oneness that is our birthright. This is why we need so much sleep at night; it requires so much psychic energy to keep the reality of Oneness at bay! That is why deep acceptance of reality is the way to weaken the ego. If we accept what is without resistance, there is no energy to keep the egoic trance going.

It is not that the ego is bad and reality is good; no such dualistic thinking is necessary. Think of it this way: the egoic identity is an evolutionary step on the way to Oneness. We can let it go any time and relax into our natural birthright. Remember Plato's Cave analogy? We have been staring at the shadows for so long, thinking that this is reality, when we just need to turn around and face the light!

One way to do this is to start thinking with the heart. Again, check out the work of the Institute of HeartMath; they have exercises to help a person regain access to the heart. The heart knows reality; the mind only knows the illusory world of its own creation. Ideally, the heart and mind work together in unison, but, the way the world is now, the mind is in complete dominance.

When we meditate, we enter the realm of the heart...and we still or quiet the mind. In so doing, we allow for peace to come into the heart. With the mind in charge, there can be no lasting peace, because the mind always has opinions about how it thinks things should be—in other words, resistance to what is. The mind naturally thinks about things, comparing them to other things, resisting what it doesn't like, moving towards what it does like, being in conflict and/or competition with what it doesn't like, and so on. You get the picture; this is called the normal human condition. But it doesn't have to be this way.

We can enter the peace of the heart by allowing in the unconditional love that is our birthright. The sun is a good metaphor for unconditional love: it shines on everything equally; it doesn't have favorites. Unconditional love is for everyone equally; no one is really special. When you have the experience of the peace of the heart in unconditional love for all life, then you can feel the current of connection between yourself and all life-forms. You can feel the current of life coursing through your heart and thereby connecting you to everything. Try this as an exercise: quiet your mind, soften your heart or emotional realm, and see if you can feel the current of connection between you and everything else. It takes some practice but it can be done, but you must get out of your mind to do it! You basically have to surrender to the grace of the heart. Then Oneness can be known.

ONENESS AND THE HEART

You will never achieve Oneness with the mind. That is why being conceptually enlightened is basically useless!

I took a nine-day training years ago called Avatar (long before the movie of the same name). While sitting on a bench and looking out at an open field, I suddenly saw that I was intimately connected to everything in the field...that it was in me! The only way to perceive Oneness is to have the experience of being connected to all life. This is where alternative reality training can be useful. Some people have this experience with hallucinogenic drugs, some with shamanic practice, some with deep meditation, some with yogic practice.

None of these are likely to produce a permanent state of Oneness but they give you the taste of it. The spiritual teacher Adyashanti calls this the "non-abiding" type of awakening experience. And, as Ken Wilber points out, an altered state can lead to a higher level of development.

There is another way to arrive at an experience of Oneness but it is not necessarily recommended. As Eckhart Tolle (*The Power of Now*) and Byron Katie (*Loving What Is*) both found out, you can get to such a point of utter despair that you drop into a state of surrender to life, and this can break the ego's hold on you. This surrender can produce a spontaneous awakening to the truth of who you are. After his awakening experience, Tolle talks about sitting on a park bench for two years, just being blissed out by the wonder of life.

Anything you can do to give yourself the experience of Oneness is, in my view, valuable. It can snap you out of the illusion of separateness. In my earlier book, *FrameShifting: A Path to Wholeness* (Loving Healing Press, 2008), I spoke of my experience of smoking very powerful marijuana for the first time. Not wanting to be ridiculed by my friends who got stoned with two joints, I smoked eight more by myself...until I felt this inexorable draw towards an abyss, and it took all my psychic power—my egoic fear—to pull me away from it, over and over. This "abyss" might have been the void that Tolle and Katie went into to achieve their breakthrough Oneness. I might have been resisting Oneness (or, more truthfully, my ego was resisting Oneness!). This went on for twelve hours. I never saw reality the same way again. However, it didn't last as a permanent experience; just a taste. I did see that I was living a very superficial life at that time.

Non-abiding awakening experiences are apparently very common. Then comes the "I got it, I lost it" experience, as Adyashanti refers to it. Think of it this way: the ego is like gravity. Unless we can get out of the gravitational field of the ego, we will be pulled back into duality and separation. It takes a certain propulsion to break out of the gravitational field of the ego. Once we get to a certain altitude (i.e., a higher level of consciousness or higher vibrational level), we can avoid this "I got it; I lost it" scenario. For most people, this seems to be the way that they achieve enlightenment and a permanent experience of Oneness; for a few, like Byron Katie and Eckhart Tolle, it can come in an instant of despair and suffering.

AN ENNEAGRAM PERSPECTIVE ON ONENESS

Again, all types are trapped in duality. But the spiritual path of the One (the Perfectionist), which is serenity, can provide the doorway through which they approach the experience of Oneness. Evolved Ones can see that all that exists has a fundamental rightness to life and that everything that has occurred is correct and perfect. But the spiritually immature One only sees error and things that are not right, both in themselves and in others. This is the perfectionist or the idealist of the Enneagram.

Ones often look bright and shiny with a clean and scrubbed quality about themselves. They are constantly trying to be good according their internal model of what good is, so they are hard on themselves and also hard on others. No one lives up to their model of perfection, least of all themselves. They often feel burdened with their criticality and intolerance of imperfection but feel at a loss to do anything about it. They can be quite controlling, trying to make others do things the right way. They are aligned with their superego and tend to be judgmental and critical, both of themselves and others.

As an Enneagram type Seven, I often find myself having a difficult time being around Ones. I have very few perfectionist tendencies myself, unless I get stressed; then I can become critical and judgmental. So watching Ones do their perfectionistic dance can bring out a lot of compassion and empathy in me because I can see my tendency under stress to do the same thing.

THE TRUE REALITY

Oneness is the true reality and the separated state is a mirage— a convincing mirage, yes, but a mirage nonetheless. Practice living in your heart. Practice living in the present moment. Practice mindfulness. Practice feeling the grace of the heart. Practice feeling the current of life coursing through you and connecting you to all life-forms. Practice meditation and experience the deep inner peace that results. The path to Oneness is either a long process of evolution (most of us) or an instantaneous awakening (Tolle and Katie noted above); either one will work!

If we continue to depend solely on our physical senses for our definitions of reality, we will be stuck in the three-dimensional trance that is the egoic state. And, as pointed out earlier, our senses are notoriously unreliable and inaccurate. In truth, we are multidimensional beings and, if we can access those other dimensions to complement our senses, we can begin to experience the joy of Oneness.

CHAPTER 8

♡

The Awakened Heart

"We love purely when we release other people to be who they are. The ego seeks intimacy through control and guilt. The Holy Spirit seeks intimacy through acceptance and release."
—Marianne Williamson, *A Return to Love*

What is an awakened heart? It is a heart filled with unconditional love for all of life. It accepts everything as it is, with no resistance or judgment of anything or anyone, including oneself! Basically it is letting go to the pulsations of life that are moving the cosmos and moving us, too. With the egoic mind in charge, we ignore the pulsations that operate the cosmos in favor of our own designs, beliefs, attitudes and compulsions. We operate as though we were God or Source. Here is the paradox: We actually *are* Source in human form (remember the Bible says we are made in the image and likeness of God?), but we can't know this fact while we are in the illusory egoic identity.

So, when I say we operate as if we were God, I mean the egoic identity, all puffed up with self-importance, tries to dictate the terms of its life experiences. It does this primarily by resisting what *is*, in favor of its conception of what *should* be (according to its opinions, beliefs, attitudes and values). The ego tries to substitute these thought forms for the direct experience of the inner urge of Spirit—what is called the still, small voice within. The ego's voice is very loud and insistent and it drowns out the still, small voice of spirit…but this voice does not go away. God, you might say, has infinite patience with us mortals, knowing that when we finally decide that the ego's guidance is very poor, we will surrender to Divine guidance!

EGO IS A STATE OF CONSCIOUSNESS—NOTHING MORE

All of the great spiritual teachings over the millennia have directed us to look within and "know thyself." Unless we know ourselves, we cannot transcend suffering in human form. In fact, it is because we do not know ourselves that we are so prone to suffering. We are also prone to misunderstanding the nature of who we are and of reality itself.

Our assumption that we are something separate, something other than everything around us, is the basis of what I call "egoic consciousness." We have spoken of this before, but I want to take it a bit deeper here. What we are talking about here is a state of consciousness, a way of packaging the world conceptually. When our mind starts to imagine that we are something separate and different from the world around us, it changes the way we perceive, which means it changes our state of consciousness. The thoughts we believe alter our state of consciousness.

What is a belief? It is a crystallized thought form, one that we have reinforced over time as our "truth." We no longer challenge its veracity. The same is true of attitudes and values, both of which are based in belief. And these thought forms are contained in "stories" about who we are, what the world is about, whether the world is dangerous or benign, and so forth. This forms what psychologists call the *self-concept*. There are good self-concepts and bad self-concepts but they all share a common denominator: an assumption that we are separate and different from the world around us.

You can observe this shift of consciousness by doing a little experiment. Imagine a sunny day on the beach. You are lying there in complete relaxation with the waves lapping at the shore. You can feel the warm sand supporting you from beneath. You can feel the rays of the sun as they warm your face. You can hear seagulls calling in the background. If you just think those thoughts and allow yourself to really feel them, they will start to change your consciousness. You will literally start feeling differently about this present moment, even though nothing has changed, even though you are not at the beach! All of it is created in your mind, through imagination, yet it can change the way you feel—and how you feel affects how you perceive yourself, others and the world around you.

So, to take it further, when your mind interprets a sense of self to mean that there actually *is* a separate self, our consciousness changes. Before long, everywhere it looks, it sees separation. Of course, it doesn't tell you this. Most humans don't walk around saying to themselves, "I feel separate from everything around me. I am distinct and different." That is because this egoic consciousness becomes so integrated in the way you see and experience life that you don't even have to remind yourself of it. You don't have to consciously think about it because it is so deeply woven in the fabric of your consciousness. The truth is that, ultimately speaking, ego is nothing but a state of consciousness...no more, no less.

If this fact was fully understood in its deepest aspect, we wouldn't be chained to the ego. We wouldn't be weighed down by it. We wouldn't feel isolated and alone in a hostile universe. Yet we do see ourselves as very separate entities, and everyone else is doing the same thing, seeing themselves as separate, different from others and from life in general. So we live in a world where almost everyone we meet reflects back to us this egoic sense of consciousness. To find liberation, we must wake up from this dream that our mind creates, that we are something separate from everything around us. This is the only way we can begin to find a way out of suffering. And this can be done with the awakened heart.

LETTING LOVE RULE

We just decide to let Love rule. It is said that the Cosmos is made of the energy of love. Remember that love and fear are the only two emotions there are; all others are variants of these two. Love is expansive; fear is contractive. So, if we let love rule, we align ourselves with the energy that is operating the whole cosmos.

We then do not need to be preoccupied with planning our lives. Planning is a substitute for *knowing* what to do next. If we align with life, we will always know what to do next because we are naturally in alignment with the energy that is running everything. What could be a better plan? Yes, we may need to look forward and plan a meal, a trip, a vacation, and so forth, but the point is this: stay connected with the pulse of Spirit so you will know when to change your plans. There is one heart that unifies humanity; let's feel it now!

You can be sure of an accurate guidance system when you listen to your heart. Have you ever had the experience of listening to your heart, knowing what to do, and then having your mind come in with its arguments and persuasion, and allowing it to change your direction? This is a common experience of many people. And you end up regretting your choice, don't you? The mind does not know what to do. It has a very limited perspective, while the heart connects you with all life, and, listening to the heart, you know exactly what to do!

You can listen to the heart in your outer world and your inner world, since they are both the same in reality. If you see a situation where you do not know what to do, get quiet inside and ask: "What would be the best thing for me to do right now for the good of the whole?" The answer will come. Similarly, if you have a question arise internally, get quiet inside, and ask the same question. Unfailingly, your heart knows exactly what to do in every situation. If your mind butts in and tries to give an opinion, just thank it for sharing and basically ignore its advice!

AN ENNEAGRAM PERSPECTIVE ON THE AWAKENED HEART

I am choosing the type that has the most difficulty having an open heart: Type Five, the Observer. Fives are mental types who find it very challenging to deal with feelings. When things get too emotionally intense, Fives tend to withdraw. They report feeling that the outer world seems to intrude on them and their space. Fives value their solitude. In fact, after stretches of sociability, they need to withdraw and recharge their batteries, so to speak. Fives value self-sufficiency and their own autonomy.

The Five is a fear type. Driven by an inner sense of scarcity and emptiness, Fives are afraid that the little they have will be taken from them by the world. The way they cope with perceived danger is to pull back. This is why a Five falling in love is taking a big risk; their defenses are not effective when they are in love. Afraid that nothing will be forthcoming from the outside, they act as though they don't want anything and are completely independent. So, for a Five to have an awakened heart, they must move into their heart and allow themselves to be vulnerable. This is a big stretch for them but can be of great value to their lives.

I know a formerly aloof Type Five who has converted to Sufism, which is the mystical branch of Islam. This sect practices a heart-opening meditation on a daily basis. I have known this Five all his life and I can say, without fear of contradiction, that his heart has opened enormously and he expresses love to most all the folks he meets. What a transformation!

CHARACTERISTICS OF THE AWAKENED HEART

Forgiveness is natural for an awakened heart. By forgiveness, I do not mean that you forgive someone for what they allegedly did to you; since everyone "out there" is part of you, no one really did anything to you. Forgiveness is merely relinquishing your judgments of another person and saying, "I release you of all judgment and bless you on your journey."

The spiritual thought system called A Course in Miracles promotes forgiveness as its primary orientation. There is a powerful mantra its followers recite to themselves when there is a forgiveness opportunity: "You are pure and innocent. All is forgiven and released." Forgiveness frees you from the negative energy of judgment and frees the other person from your condemnation, which is also a negative thought form. To forgive is good for everyone! Radical acceptance as forgiveness is the way to go.

Compassion and empathy are also natural for the awakened heart. Compassion is saying to another, "I have had difficulties in my life, so I know how you must feel." Again, this is not to be confused with enabling, which sees the other person as a victim and you as the rescuer. That helps no one. Empathy is similar to compassion; here you are trying on the other's shoes, so to speak, and walking in them. This is a way for you to experience what it must be like to be that person. Both empathy and compassion acknowledge, in a very specific way, the Oneness of all life. If you can really understand what that so-called other person must be thinking, feeling and experiencing, then you can be them, at least for a moment.

Imagine living in the world described in the Vision Alignment Project, where "we have all learned to pause for a moment and take a breath or two before levying a judgment upon those around us; where we take the time to put ourselves in the other person's shoes long enough to see life from their perspective, and then to put our attention on the other person the way they would want that attention put on them. Likewise, imagine a world where we are all taught, from the time we are young children, to put ourselves in the shoes of the other person and to withhold our judgments and opinions of them. We do this because we have learned that as we do unto others we are also doing unto ourselves—and consequently, we treat our fellow travelers with a greater respect, the kind of respect we would want for ourselves should we be in the same situation." (http://www.visionalignmentproject.com/translations/vap94.html)

Loving kindness is also part of an awakened heart. Realizing that we are all part of a unified whole, we easily extend love to parts of ourselves that appear to be out there. When asked what his religion was, His Holiness the Dalai Lama said, "My religion is kindness." Loving kindness is a natural attitude when you experience yourself as part of the whole. In the separated egoic state, loving kindness is a rare occurrence because our minds are constantly judging what is good and what is bad—and with judgment comes condemnation and blame, not loving kindness.

LIVING WITH AN AWAKENED HEART

If you are living with an awakened heart, you automatically have an attitude of sacred service, gratitude, compassion and forgiveness...because you realize that everything that appears to be separate from you is really you! You wisely decide to extend to yourself the loving kindness that is the birthright of all sentient life.

An awakened heart is not judgmental or critical for the same reason. An awakened heart lives in the present moment and spontaneously knows what to do as it rests in the current that is moving the galaxies. It feels safe and secure in the awareness of its Oneness with all life. There is nothing factually to fear at all. The awakened heart is a blessing to all life.

And being a blessing is the ultimate spiritual goal. This goes beyond doing no harm. What could be simpler? But, if you are in the ego's grip, being a blessing and loving kindness are the last things on your mind. You want to get even with those folks who wronged you; you don't want to help anyone else because life seems hard and cruel, and so on. This, again, is the magician's trick of the ego, designed to keep you in bondage. Compassion, empathy and forgiveness are the last things on your mind. You are looking to make a preemptive strike against those who might harm you. Nations do this, too; nations are composed of egoic beings who want to strike out against the cruel and unfeeling world.

We must break this cycle of recrimination and revenge. The way out is the awakened heart. Once you know who you really are, a being of Spirit (not merely a body, mind or emotions), you begin to automatically see the world as part of you. You are an eternal Being of Light, not an ego living in fear of a threatening world. Live this reality and be an actual blessing to your world.

CHAPTER 9

♡

Living in Love

"The closer we grow to our inner light, the more we feel the natural urge to share that light with others.... The meaning of work, whatever its form, is that it be used to heal the world.... Love is the most powerful fuel in any endeavor. The most important question to ask about any work is 'How does this serve the world?'"
—Marianne Williamson, *Illuminata*

The subtitle of this book is *Living With an Awakening Heart*. What does that actually mean? Spiritual traditions acknowledge the heart as central to genuine human transformation. But what causes or expedites a change of heart or an awakening heart?

When we notice our heart suffering, created by deep inner discontent, we begin to come home to ourselves. The heart suffers when it is constantly being bombarded by conflicting messages from the dualistic mind: this is good, this is bad, I love this, I hate this, and so on. This discord creates inner turmoil.

Using the Enneagram typology as a reference point, we see that there are nine passions or fixations of the heart, each of which can cause us grief and suffering. By self-observation of the passion acting out its particular habitual pattern, we can study the symptoms and sources of suffering, and move towards the virtues of spiritual maturity and presence. As noted earlier, duality causes suffering by its basic nature. If our minds are constantly categorizing things as good or bad, worthwhile or worthless, and so on, this creates emotional reactions in us and turbulence is the result.

SELF-CREATED SUFFERING

Here we see the basic problem. By allowing the ego and its dualistic perceptions to rule us, we automatically create our own suffering. When we let go to the innate wisdom of the heart, our inner guide will let us know what to do in every moment, and, when we trust this guidance system, there is no need to categorize anything at all. Things aren't good or bad; they simply are the way they are. And, since we are the ones who attracted them to ourselves, we need to take one hundred percent responsibility for them...those we judge good and those we judge bad! Here is the path to inner realization, tranquility and patience. You have no doubt heard the expression "Let go and let God." Well, it happens to be wise advice. But the ego is trying to convince you that letting go is a bad strategy, that you must listen to its fearful interpretations of the outer world and protect yourself from danger.

THE MOVIE OF YOUR LIFE

A useful metaphor says looking at reality through the lens of the ego is like watching a movie. The projector of your mind is creating the movie out there and then you allow your emotions to tell you if something is good or bad. My wife and I had a graphic experience of this recently. We have been watching the PBS Masterpiece Classic *Downton Abbey* series. It is basically a nighttime soap opera, and it is well-acted and scripted. Watching this, we saw how easy it was for us to identify with the characters' plights and get emotionally involved. This is basically no different from watching one's own egoic reality and emotionally reacting to that movie!

But if you live in love, then the egoic projections diminish or stop. Emotional reactions lessen or cease. You have the assurance of the present moment. You have the faith that what you need in any situation will be provided. All the wisdom you need is available to you right now. You aren't emotionally invested in the future because it is imaginary. You don't need to regret the past; the past doesn't exist, either! These are just thought forms created by the egoic mind, trying to protect you from a supposedly hostile world out there. But the only "out there" is what our mind creates to cause us to react to it. We basically are reacting to our own fear-based creations, and then we wonder why we cannot find peace.

LIVING IN LOVE MEANS SERVING THE WHOLE

Living in love means doing that which benefits the larger whole, not just oneself. I had a strong experience of this after I wrote my book *FrameShifting: A Path to Wholeness* (Loving Healing Press, 2008). As I was preparing to go on a book tour to promote the book, I was called to attend a county board meeting where they were debating whether or not to allow a 3,500-head pig farm in our area (a concentrated animal feeding operation, or CAFO—a factory farm). A number of experts, from veterinarians to doctors to epidemiologists and others, came to testify how bad it would be from a health standpoint. On the opposite side, a few farmers got up and said, "You can't tell me what to do with my land," but the testimony was overwhelmingly anti-CAFO.

At the end of the testimony, the twenty-nine supervisors took a vote, and, to my shock, the vote was twenty-six to three in favor of allowing the CAFO to be built! Hadn't they heard the testimony? I heard later that representatives of large agri-business interests had called each representative and told them that if they blocked the CAFO, they would be sued by these companies and it could bankrupt the county in legal fees to defend their position. So the board was intimidated.

Once this happened, I felt called by the inner voice to run for a county board seat. I did and became the representative for my district. In my two years of service, a number of us so-called progressives on the board and a number of community activists were successful in blocking the hog farm and also stopping a local power plant from dumping its coal tailings (which contained arsenic and other toxic minerals) into an open pit where they could leach into the ground and ruin our drinking water. So it was definitely worth it, from the perspective of the whole, for me to run and help influence board decisions for those two years.

In 2010, when I resigned from the board, I finally did my delayed book tour, but the energy around the book was no longer what it had been. I sold a mere 38 books despite traveling to seven states and driving over 3,500 miles. The book had grown cold in the interim because I chose to stay local with meetings and committees for the board rather than travel to promote the book. Nonetheless, I am glad I ran for office and was able to contribute to our community.

Here is an example of listening to the voice of Spirit. My ego wanted me to get out there and sell that book! I had some radio interviews and the book was selling. But winning a board seat and staying in Viroqua (and not promoting the book) allowed it to go cold. Is this good or bad? Hard to know, isn't it? I did what I did. And I am pleased that this CAFO did not get built and that the toxic tailings from the coal-fired plant went into asphalt for re-covering streets, rather than being dumped into an open pit. This does not make me a local hero; I just did what Spirit prompted me to do for the good of the whole.

AN ENNEAGRAM PERSPECTIVE ON LIVING IN LOVE

For this perspective, I have chosen the Type Three—the Achiever or the Performer. Being an image type, Threes have, as their passion, deceit; this primarily means that they come to think they *are* their image and they want everyone else to believe that, too. Their role becomes their identity. They can be like chameleons, adapting to please every audience. As a quintessential image type, they have an overriding concern with how they present themselves to their audience. They are driven and goal-oriented; they are often called "human doers." They often drive themselves unmercifully in pursuit of goal accomplishment. As children, they learned they would get rewarded for what they achieved, rather than loved for who they are.

Threes are pragmatic, matter-of-fact, and calculating, and they possess a steely determination to do whatever it takes to get the job done. For the Three to live in love, they must confront their basic lie: *that they are what they do.* Since they get so much applause for what they do, it can be tough for them to give this up. But to live authentically in love, they must give up their image and become real. I have a great deal of admiration for Threes who give up the applause and commit to living life with authenticity.

THINKING WITH THE HEART

In Chapter 7, I introduced the idea of thinking with the heart. What does this mean? Science has now shown us that the heart actually does think, albeit in a different way than the mind. And if the mind and the heart can be in communion with each other, that is the perfect scenario. Those with eyes to see can admit that thinking with the mind alone has gotten us god-awful nowhere, except of course, living in hell. It turns out that hell is not some place other than right here, right now; and if you are willing to let your mind rule, that is a worthy definition of hell on earth.

Let us revisit the proposition that resistance to what is enables the ego to strengthen itself. So why does the ego resist what is? Because it always wants more, or different, or better in some way that it is in comparison to the present state. Things are rarely the way the ego wants them; have you noticed that yet? So we could say that resistance to life is the modus operandi of the ego. And if we just are willing to accept things the way they, even love them the way they are, then the ego has no food with which to sustain itself. Many New Age folks would have us destroy the ego; however, as long as we are inhabiting bodies, this will probably not be possible. The mind actually creates the body, moment by moment. But we can consciously weaken the ego and eventually integrate it into our larger Self or Higher Self.

Let me relate an example in my life of non-resistance to what is. There is a difference between *loving* what is and *accepting* what is; for the purposes of this book, I am going to propose that both strategies work! When I was twenty-five years old, I had some very serious back surgery; I had what is called a double lumbar laminectomy (two discs in my lower back were partially removed). I knew nothing about surgery or about the orthopedic surgeon, who did ten of these surgeries every day. Six weeks after the surgery, I was so stiff that I could not bend over at the waist. So I went in to see him. Sitting in the waiting room, a very pleasant lady asked me, "Are you doing your exercises?" I replied, "What exercises?" Apparently the doctor was supposed to have given me some rehabilitative exercises to do to keep my back from stiffening up.

Furious, I went into his office and confronted him: "What is this about exercises?" He replied, "Oh, I must have forgotten to give them to you." He said I must do them now to break loose the adhesions that had formed in my back. I did them—and my back went into spasm. I had to wear a cast for six months to keep my back straight. Even after I took it off, my back was in constant pain. Clearly, back then, I was not loving it all; I was into victimization and blame.

Looking for sympathy, I complained to everyone about my back, even total strangers! After a while, I got tired of listening to myself whine, so I decided to just accept it as it was and live my life. Then an interesting thing happened. About three months later, I noticed it didn't hurt anymore! This taught me the spiritual principle that *whatever you pay attention to expands*. By not paying attention to the pain and just accepting it as it was, I allowed it to dissipate.

THE STAYING POWER OF THE EGO

You can be sure that ego will not give up its dominance over your life without a fight. It is a cunning trickster and will resort to all manner of trickery to convince you to resist what is. It wants to maintain its dominance over you and over your experience of the world.

One could say that the major focus of the ego is the external world. That is why Jesus supposedly said "I am not of the world" (John 17:14). He lived in the world but was not moved by the world's temptations, aversions, and so forth. He was above it all. When we take the world seriously, we give weight to the illusion that the mind creates. As I've said before, we live in a mind-made world. Given that fact, the only wise strategy is to love it all, accept it all, with zero resistance to anything. Now, I am not saying that a person who is victimized or the target of domestic violence should just accept that; no, they should take responsibility for their situation and do what they can to change it.

We can consciously allow life to manifest what it will by aligning ourselves with our Divine Purpose. Just like the different organs of the body have a purpose, so do we as cells of the cosmic whole. If we follow the guidance of Cosmic Will, we are sure to live lives of fulfillment and joy. Does this mean there will be no bumps along the way? Not at all; our soul has chosen a life path for each of us and that path might include some uncomfortable moments (or years!). But here is where trust in life and its purposes come in. If we trust the guidance of life itself, and put the ego in its place (in the background), then we can be assured that our lives will have meaning and value.

LIVING IN LOVE

So what would living in love look like? Well, for starters, it would mean that fear would dissipate from your experience. There would be nothing to fear since you would express unconditional love for all life. Therefore, you would not attract to yourself anything that might seek to harm you. You have cleared out all of your shadow so there is no unconscious material to attract hurtful circumstances. You would naturally extend to everyone and everything an unconditional love that will be the light of the world. You would see everything as a natural extension of your Self. You would give of yourself freely in sacred service because you would know that you are part of One Cosmic Whole. You would often have a smile on your face; joy for absolutely no reason would be a common occurrence. And you would give thanks for all things, even those things that you might have judged bad or wrong in the past; now you would see them as indicators of your evolved nature and a reminder of the need for humility and openness.

So the overall message of this book is just what the title says. Loving it all means to love everything that comes to you because it is showing you your unhealed shadow aspects as well as your loving intent and gratitude. Everything that is contained in your mind can and will be projected onto the screen of your life experience. Love it all; this way the ego cannot gain a foothold on your emotions and your satisfaction. By resisting nothing, we accept life as it is, and allow for the clarification that comes with surrendering to the One Spirit that is animating the entire cosmos! This is the way to contentment and perfect joy.

CHAPTER 10

♡

Using the Enneagram to Transcend Duality

"God's will is that we be happy. God's will is that we forgive
ourselves. God's will is that we find our place in Heaven now."
—Marianne Williamson, *A Course in Miracles* calendar, May 8.

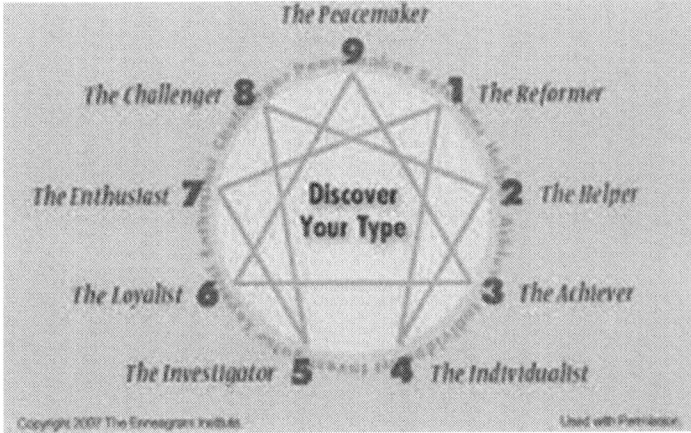

A long time ago, the human mind decided that it could judge what to accept as good and what to reject; what to take responsibility for and what to deny responsibility for. This has been referred to as eating of the fruit of the tree of the knowledge of good and evil. The result is what we call egoic consciousness, and this division between acceptable and unacceptable is what creates the illusion of separation. If we only receive what we like and we deny responsibility for what we do not like, this leads to blame and the placing of responsibility seemingly outside ourselves. But in reality we are all one, so blaming another person for what you do not like is factually blaming yourself.

When this state of mind is taken to extremes, as we see today, lots of folks suffer depression, despair and hopelessness. Moment by moment throughout our day, we see a world based on the principle of separation, and all our choices and actions arise from that false view. Another way of putting this is that we have been listening to the wrong voice—the voice of the ego instead of the voice of Spirit.

The egoic voice wants you to like some things and dislike others; to see some things as good and some things as bad. In so doing, you get to take 100 percent responsibility for what you like but blame others for what you don't like! When we adopt a consciousness of separation, we automatically move into conflict and dis-ease. We then see others as either threats or enhancements to self, but never as one with oneself.

You will *never* get to a realization of oneness with all life through the counsel of the ego. It is impossible, because the ego is committed to seeing the world as a dangerous, hostile place where its counsel is the only way to safety and security. Resistance to "what is" is the modus operandi of the ego. But it is possible to cultivate just the opposite: to look with innocence, as a child does, at whatever arises in your field of experience. It is even possible to look at your own emotions from a stance of curiosity and wonder, as you might look at a cloud that passes in the sky. You simply notice it, marvel at it, appreciate it, and let it pass by.

Thoughts and feelings are like passing clouds. The ego wants to grab them, make them significant, and reinforce its identity by believing them. Our so-called problems come mainly from believing our thoughts and defending our feelings. When we do this, we give them weight as though they were actually real.

This is where meditation is especially useful. To stop thinking and just let everything be as it is might sound simple, but you'll find that the mind is always telling you to know more, to be more, to do something. All of this endless mind chatter keeps us bound in the egoic perspective. To let go to the mystery of life means to stop the incessant, automatic thinking. And in meditation, you begin to see how hard this is to do. We are so deeply conditioned to believe what our minds and emotions tell us to believe. There are layers and layers of conditioned thought and belief in all of us. Loving it all helps us experience all of these layers as we continually let go to how things actually are.

The ego believes that its identity depends on its thinking, perceptions, feelings and experiences, so it thinks that if it lets go of them it will die. The ego therefore counsels us to grip, to hold on to these things. If they were physical objects, our knuckles would be turning white, trying to hold on to our limitations, guilt, unworthiness and doubt. But living in the state of loving it all requires openness, trust, expansiveness and spaciousness. It involves allowing, trusting in that small, still voice of your Source, witnessing and letting things come and go. It also involves learning to cultivate a deep enjoyment of whatever arises, seeing that all things are simply an aspect of oneself in truth, so they can be let go of when it is time to do so.

MASTERY ARISES FROM PURE INNOCENCE

The world of unworthiness, conflict, despair, fear and guilt and the world of pure bliss lie side by side in your own mind. What you must learn to do is cultivate the innocence that a child carries before it is socialized with fear and separation thoughts. This is why Jesus is said to have taught that we must "become as little children" (Matthew 18:3) to enter the kingdom of heaven. The way to Oneness is to consciously cultivate the attitude of wonder and openness of a little child.

Now, you might be thinking this sounds naïve. What about all those evil people out there in the world who want to hurt you? If there are people out there who wants to hurt you, that means there is more work to do in your consciousness to integrate these shadow elements.

Innocence is not the same as naïveté. Innocence is pure un-judging defenselessness, no guard up for the dangers of the so-called evil external world.

All of us have an archetype of separation, as depicted by the nine personality types described by the Enneagram. Each of these types begins as an aspect of God-essence, but some kind of trauma occurs in childhood and the person moves from *wanting* to exemplify that essence to *having* to exemplify it. This is called a fixation. Let me explain.

USING THE ENNEAGRAM TO DEVELOP COMPASSION AND EMPATHY

This tool called the Enneagram is a perfect method to develop your compassion and empathy towards yourself and towards others. Why? Because when you know which type is fixated in your consciousness, you can begin to catch yourself doing the habitual behavior of the specific fixation.

If you are, in fact, one with everything, then each fixation is contained in you. Begin to recognize that the other person is just doing their type. It is nothing personal—they are not trying to irritate you or hurt you. They are just acting habitually as the type would dictate. You react to it because it is not what you want them to do. And this type is contained in you! It looks like the other person, but, as you develop more and more awareness of yourself as the other, you will feel yourself acting in all these ways.

The more you experience yourself acting as an Enneagram type, the more clearly you will see that none of it is personal. All of the Enneagram types are just habitual personality patterns of thought, feeling and behavior. This becomes easy to see when one is in the observer position of watching the type unfold.

TYPE ONE: THE PERFECTIONIST

Take the archetype of the Type One, the Perfectionist or the Idealist. This person begins by exemplifying the aspect of God called *goodness*; God is good. So the young One child begins by *wanting* to be good; then this wanting becomes solidified as *having* to be good. Often, Ones have a parent or parents who are also Ones, so this "getting it right" starts early. It becomes a compulsion or an addiction. Ones are naturally drawn to what is wrong in their environment, to error. In a room that is new to them, they will immediately spot the place on the wall where the paint dripped, the stain on the rug, and so on.

In Enneagram language, this is called a fixation. In other words, the ego grabs this God-essence and makes it into a fixed part of the personality. Type One people feel that they must be good all the time, so they beat themselves up for their supposed failures—and they can also be hard on others. Here is how the ego co-opts the God-essence that comes in with the DNA and makes it into a personality structure that is guaranteed to bring pain, conflict and dissatisfaction.

To overcome this fixation, if you are a Type One, you can begin to cultivate a sense that "this is good enough." You can begin to consciously cut yourself some slack. Now, your ego will not like this since it is looking to resist. So when your mind argues, "This is not good enough!" you can gently say to it, "Thank you for sharing, but I want to see the world with innocent eyes." If you are not a Type One, you can begin to develop empathy towards that persona and how hard they are on themselves (and, usually, on others).

The One is part of the anger triad on the Enneagram of Eight, Nine, One. All three of these types are motivated by anger but they express it differently. All three are also called body or instinctual types, meaning that they make decisions based on their gut feelings. Now, Ones often don't seem angry, but they sometimes can be resentful. Resentful of what? They can be resentful of all those other people who aren't working as hard as *they* are to be good! The One can get so resentful that they really lose it and flare up in anger; then they feel terrible because losing it is not good or perfect or "right."

So another thing you can do if you are a Type One is to take a vacation! Ones need a respite from their ultra-responsible attitude towards life. They need to play! The spiritual goal for the One is *serenity*. Ones need to remind themselves that this is their goal: to be serene, to let up on their hard-driving goal of getting it done "right," according to their internal standards of correctness.

TYPE TWO: THE HELPER OR THE GIVER

The archetype of Type Two is the Giver or the Helper. This person comes in with the God-essence of *giving* or *helping* (God is a giver). They start off by wanting to help, but they quickly learn that being a helper means they get a lot of positive strokes for their help. They then decide they *have* to help so that they can be seen as indispensable and therefore will be valued by others. Here is the fixation of the Two; they *have* to help and, of course, they deny their own needs in the process.

Twos are like chameleons: they adapt to whoever needs their help, and they are quite good at it. Here again the ego co-opts the God-given need to help others and the Two bases their sense of worth on being a compulsive helper. If there is no one to give to, the Two feels quite lost and adrift; this is why many Two mothers have such a hard time with empty nest syndrome. Their sense of self-worth is tied up with helping others.

The Two, Three and Four compose the so-called image triad on the Enneagram. These are called the feeling or heart types of the Enneagram; they make decisions with their emotions. All three of these types have adopted an image to receive appreciation and, they hope, love from others. The Two develops the image of the indispensable helper so they can win love. But beneath the surface on all the image types is the feeling that they are a phony. As a result, all three types also have a basic self-hatred.

If you are Type Two, you can begin to cultivate of sense of "I have needs, too." Of course, this is very hard for the Two to do, since their ego screams that this is selfish. The passion (or the energy underlying the type) of the Two is *pride*. Now, if you ask a Two if they feel proud, they will look at you strangely. They are not conscious of their pride; it is a hidden passion. But Twos feel like they are the best givers in the world: "No one can take care of others' needs like I can!" This is pride, pure and simple. The spiritual task for the two is *humility*. Twos need to admit not only that their sense of identity isn't just their ability to help others, but also that they themselves need help sometimes. Actually, Twos are the most co-dependent of all the Enneagram types.

If the Two gives and gives, and does not receive what they consider to be adequate attention and appreciation, they get stressed out and can get quite angry. But if they feel really comfortable in their own skin, they can resort to creative endeavors and feel less compulsive about being the constant giver.

TYPE THREE: THE ACHIEVER OR THE PERFORMER

The God-essence that comes in with this archetype is *efficiency* and *performance*. Threes are successful people, and, of course, God is successful. Threes are the "doers" of the Enneagram; if you want a job completed, give it to a Three! As children, Threes got rewarded for getting things done. So at first they *want* to get things done and accomplish goals, but as the fixation sets in they feel they *must* be successful. As a result, most Threes are successful—and if they aren't, they tend to reframe it as a learning experience.

Threes are the people with no space in their Day-Timers. They are feeling types but they tend to use up all their feeling energy with performance; so, quite often, they feel nothing at all (while the Twos and Fours are hyper-feeling types). Threes are always busy. If you ask a Three to just come hang out with you, it makes them nervous. If they aren't doing something and accomplishing goals, they get quite uncomfortable. They feel like they are not earning their worthiness.

The passion of the Three is *deceit*. They are basically deceiving themselves by thinking that they *are* their goal accomplishment and their success, and they deceive others in the same way. The spiritual path for the Three is *honesty*. If a Three can really get in touch with their essential worth independent of their success, they can begin to heal their egoic trance.

If the Three works and works and burns out (which they are quite susceptible to doing), they collapse in a heap until they can recharge their batteries and get going again. But, as the Three feels more comfortable and learns to practice self-honesty, they can develop a sense of loyalty towards others, a healthy skepticism and mental clarity.

TYPE FOUR: THE TRAGIC ROMANTIC

The God-essence of the Four archetype is *uniqueness* (God is unique). Fours are very unique people, often quite artistic. These are people who long for what they think is missing in their lives. Fours often experience melancholy and sometimes depression as they feel others don't understand or appreciate them. The passion of the Four is *envy*. Fours tend to see others as having what they themselves do not have. This is not the same as jealousy—they don't want to take it from you; they just wish they had it too (whatever "it" is).

Fours are people who get attention by being unique in their expression. They are "meaning-junkies" in the sense that their focus is on what things mean at their deepest essence. They are *not* superficial people. Also, they tend to be drama queens and kings; they look for and create situations that tend towards the tragic.

Low self-esteem is a problem for all the types, but especially for Fours. Even as they seek to be creative in their expression and their work, there is an underlying sense of "I am not good enough; this is why I have been abandoned in my life." Abandonment is a central issue for the type Four.

Fours experience great mood swings, from the depths of melancholy to the heights of great joy and back down again. So the spiritual path for the four is *equanimity,* balancing out their up and down moods.

TYPE FIVE: THE OBSERVER

The God-essence of the Five archetype is *omniscience* (God is all-knowing). All the types develop a survival strategy in their early years to stay safe in a potentially hostile world. For Ones, it is being right. For Twos, it is being the best helper. For Threes, it is getting the job done. For Fours, it is being unique. And for Fives, it is knowing everything about a certain subject so they can be the expert. And Fives, being mental types, are usually quite smart.

Fives are called the Observer because they usually are quite introverted and tend to withdraw to stay safe. They prefer to stay in the background and watch what is going on. They are one of the fear types and withdrawal is their way to stay safe.

When Fives feel safe, they can draw on the power and energy of the type Eight. They can even get up in front of a group and present a topic! But too much "people contact" is hard for Fives; they periodically need to withdraw and recharge their batteries, so to speak.

Fives tend towards *avarice* (their passion). They start out *wanting* to know everything; they fixate on *having* to know everything. The avarice comes in concerning their knowledge; Fives tend to hold on to their knowledge unless they really trust you. They are stingy with what they know. Fives tend to be secretive, again to protect their knowledge, which is their measure of self-worth. But they are very competent people and really good at completing tasks, especially if they are tasks that can be done alone.

The spiritual path for the Five is *non-attachment*. What this means is that they need to loosen up their grasp on what they know and let it flow to others freely.

TYPE SIX: THE LOYAL SKEPTIC

The God-essence of the Six is *loyalty* (God is loyal to his people). Sixes are the core fear type. They try to prepare for any eventuality beforehand. Their motto is "Be prepared." Usually, this stems from an unpredictable childhood experience, such as alcoholism or mental illness in the family. So the Six child goes from *wanting* to be safe to *having* to be safe. The chief passion of the Six archetype is *doubt*; Sixes tend to be skeptical of people and situations. They can also be worriers, wanting to overprepare for anything that might happen.

The Six is the only type that has two versions to it: the phobic and the counterphobic. The phobic Six is just afraid and always seeks to anticipate anything bad that might happen. The counterphobic Six, on the other hand, tends to move towards any perceived danger as a way of coping with their fear. They tend to look brave but they are just as afraid as the phobic Six. Gordon Liddy of Watergate fame is probably a counterphobic Six. In his autobiography, he brags about dealing with his fear of rodents by catching a rat, cooking and eating part of it.

The passion of the Six is *fear*. The spiritual path is *courage*. This is true courage, not the reactionary courage described in the Gordon Liddy example. Sixes are good, loyal friends; the type is also called the Trooper. Sixes are also great problem-solvers; they love a tough problem. Being mental types, they are quick to solve them.

TYPE SEVEN: THE EPICURE

The Seven is also part of the fear triad (Five, Six, Seven) but they don't appear afraid at all! Sevens are optimistic, creative, ready for adventure and spontaneous in their nature. They are also usually quite social. But they do fear two things: boredom and pain. The Seven tends to "future-trip" when things get painful; they tend to leave the present moment and imagine a future time when there is no pain and lots of fun. Sevens are fun-junkies.

The God-essence of the Seven is *joy* (God is joyful). The passion of the Seven is *gluttony*. While this word can refer to food addiction, in the case of the Seven it usually means a gluttony for experience. Sevens want to try everything; that is why they are called epicures.

Immature Sevens can be quite superficial and dance around problems and potential pain. Sevens are usually the life of the party and they are often seen as party-animals. It seems like Sevens can skate ahead of possible pain by moving quickly. Robert Preston in *The Music Man* is the caricature of the Seven: come into a town, get everyone organized, put on a show and then leave town just as quickly.

Sevens can be great friends but you have to pin them down to get things done. If they get bored, they tend to impulsively switch to another thing to do. But they certainly can be fun to be around! They tend towards superficiality and this can be quite unnerving to a serious type like a One or Four.

The spiritual path for the Seven is *sobriety*; again, not necessarily sobriety relative to addictive substances but sobriety in terms of excessive future-tripping and trying a little of everything.

TYPE EIGHT: THE BOSS OR THE PROTECTOR

The God-essence of the Eight is *power* (God is powerful). The Eight is part of the anger triad described earlier (Eight, Nine, One), but unlike the One, Eights can explode with anger and not feel the least bit guilty about it! In fact, they *love* a good argument! They love conflict and a good fight.

The passion of the Eight is *lust*; they want more of everything. These are people with big energy; they can get things done and are almost impossible to wear out! Young Eights, when they saw the big people around them who appeared not to know what they were doing, decided to make up their own rules. These are the outlaws (nonconformists) of the Enneagram. The rules are for everyone else! They march to their own drummer and make up their own rules for living. As a result, you will find some of them in jail from time to time.

Eight, besides being strong, lustful people, can also be protectors of the downtrodden and meek. In fact, if an Eight sees someone being bullied, they will likely take out the bully. This is why they are called the Protector in addition to being the Boss. My daughter is an Eight. When she was a child, her friends included a girl with cerebral palsy and a Hispanic child, and if anyone teased them, she would stand up for them and rebuke the tormentor.

The Eight's orientation is power, but when they feel comfortable, they can also be remarkably caring and giving people. Under stress, though, they tend to withdraw and sort of give up for a while.

The spiritual path for the Eight is *innocence*. They need to recover their lost innocence from childhood when they felt they had to be strong and run things.

TYPE NINE: THE MEDIATOR OR THE PEACEMAKER

Type Nine has a God-essence of *peace* (God is peaceful). Nines are calm, mellow people who tend to go with the flow. They really hate conflict and they have a great gift in being able to understand other points of view, but they tend to lose their own view. Nines have great trouble identifying what they want.

The passion for the Nine is called *sloth* or laziness. They are an anger type (part of the anger triad) but they rarely let themselves get angry, primarily because they hate conflict. So when anger rises up in them, they tend to get sleepy; hence the sloth caricature. They literally go to sleep on their anger.

Nines are often procrastinators and they often are late to meetings or other appointments. They are typically not initiators or entrepreneurs; they make good followers rather than leaders.

Nines are wonderful peacemakers and they are very good at helping others see alternative points of view. They make great counselors and therapists.

The spiritual path for the Nine is called *right action*. What this means is that when they finally can identify what they want, they need to *do it*—they need to take action.

TOWARDS ONESELF: USING THE ENNEAGRAM AS A TOOL FOR SELF-DISCOVERY

Why is all this important? Because when you can watch yourself "do your type" from a conscious viewpoint, you can choose another response besides the habitual one dictated by the type structure. When you feel yourself being sucked into the grip of the type, try deep belly breathing until the contraction into the habit pattern loosens. Once the type has you in its grip, it is pretty hard to not follow it out. This is what Eckhart Tolle calls the "pain body" working itself into your consciousness. The ego holds a lot of pain from the past (as well as from past lives). But if you can catch it early on, when you feel the contraction of the type coming on, and breathe into your belly, it will subside.

Two of my Enneagram teachers, Don Riso and Russ Hudson, authors of *The Wisdom of the Enneagram*, say that there is a developmental cycle for each type; in other words, there can be an undeveloped Seven, an average Seven, and an enlightened Seven, and they all look different. They all have the same, common Seven characteristics, but the more developed levels are more aware of their habitual tendencies and can choose to behave differently.

Oneness dawns when each of us can watch ourselves as the observer of our thoughts, attitudes and behavior. This is the precursor to full enlightenment. One moves from the unconscious, reactive egoic self into the awakened Self. It is not that the ego is bad; it is just a poor guide for your life. Its view is from the separated self, and, by definition, it cannot see the whole picture. With an awakened heart, you see with compassion and empathy for all beings that are seemingly different from you.

The quickest way to Oneness is to love it all. The egoic tendency, as I said earlier, is to accept responsibility for what you like and to blame others or the circumstance for what you don't like. The fact is that you created it all and therefore the only sane thing to do is accept responsibility for it all. By loving it all, you open your heart, forgive yourself, feel grateful for your entire life and develop clear and penetrating awareness of reality. What could be better than that?

Epilogue

Have you ever wondered why, with all the solutions offered, with all the government programs, with the law enforcement agencies, courts, lawyers, and so forth, trying their best, things seem to be getting worse all the time? Have you ever noticed that, with every solution offered for a problem, there are usually unintended consequences? Think of suburbia and traffic congestion, industrialization and pollution, antibiotics and the rise of drug-resistant microbes, and many other examples. With all the bright people in the world, why is there still imminent social, economic, political and environmental collapse?

The answer to all these questions is the same: until we can determine that a proposed solution to a problem will have only life-enhancing outcomes, we will continue to grope our way around in the dark, trying to solve problems with limited understanding of the solution's impact on the whole. Plato said many years ago, in his wonderful allegory, that we are like people who live in a cave. In this cave is a fire, and shadows are thrown onto the wall from the light of the fire. We are facing the shadows and believe that they are reality. Until we turn around and face the light, we will continue to stumble around with the best intentions and produce more and more unintended consequences.

From birth, we have all constructed a mind-made fiction called the ego. We construct this fiction because we feel dependent on our caregivers, separate from the whole, and we need them in order to feel safe and secure. So we construct a self that has a survival strategy. In this book, I've shown how the nine ego styles of the Enneagram embody these strategies. The ego is a false self that pretends to be separate from the whole of interconnected life and wants to "do its own thing," to maximize its pleasure and minimize its pain. This self typically ignores its connection to all life and barrels ahead, seeking personal satisfaction without considering the impact of its actions on the larger whole.

Experts in the physical sciences, including such authors as Capra, Bohm and Wilber, now agree that life is an interconnected whole. This is not a new concept—it has been a staple belief of Buddhism and Hinduism for centuries. There is also agreement that there is an inherent design to all life-forms. An acorn planted will always grow into an oak tree, never a mimosa. One could call this the Divine Design of life. But the egoic consciousness knows very little of this design. This is why actions taken from the egoic perspective will often produce unintended results. The mind, by itself, knows very little and it definitely does not know about the workings of the vast intelligence that is animating the entire cosmos!

Aside from assuming that it is separate from all life, the egoic self makes another, equally damaging assumption: it assumes that there are things it likes (that will produce pleasure) and things it dislikes (that will produce discomfort). This is called dualistic thought, and it occurs when the isolated human ego wants to get what it wants and avoid what it doesn't want. But everything that appears to be outside of us is actually produced inside of us first. We are projecting a reality that appears to be outside of us that conforms to our belief systems, attitudes and values about life (all of which are created in our past).

As small children, we begin the process of socialization, whereby we learn what is expected of us. We listen to the authority figures—our parents, religious figures, teachers, the media, the military—and we soak all of this in. This creates the lens or paradigm through which we perceive so-called reality. But what we perceive is *not* reality; it is a mind-made projection of our inner beliefs, attitudes, values, assumptions and expectations based on those beliefs. So we are experiencing a mind-made world and then reacting to that projection by liking some things that show up and disliking other things.

Resistance to what it doesn't like is the ego's way of strengthening it-self, maintaining its separate identity. Allowing everything that comes to us with love, acceptance and without resistance weakens the ego's hold on our consciousness.

Part of the ego is what Jung and Robert Bly, among others, have called the shadow. The shadow is made up of parts of our experience that produced pain or caused displeasure (and therefore rejection) in our significant others when we did something. Because we are so depen-dent on our caregivers for love and approval in our early years, we learn to stuff down those so-called unacceptable parts of ourselves. But they don't go away. They show up in our external reality as people we don't like or situations that remind us unconsciously of those events that we repressed as children. Until we can feel the pain of this repressed mate-rial, it will continue to haunt us in the present.

Another thing the ego does is take us out of the present moment by dwelling on the past and projecting into the future. Both of these are mind-made fantasies. The past is gone, and our memories are notorious for distorting what actually happened in the past; and the future is a dream—it is not here yet. So regrets about the past and fears or antici-pation about the future are just thought-forms and are not real. What is real is what is *here and now.*

Here we are in our predicament. We live from a false self that is based on the fiction of separateness from the rest of life, relying on our past experience to guide our present action and upon our judgments about what is good and what is bad. We do not actually see reality as it is; we see a projection from our inner consciousness based on our experiences and beliefs from the past. So we create our own reality and then react to it by saying we like that and we don't like that...when it all is from us!

The premise I have sought to convey in this book is that to move beyond the separatist egoic consciousness, we need to embrace and love

111

everything that comes to us—*everything*. Why? Because we created it! By taking 100 percent personal responsibility for our own worlds, we tell the truth about our experience. If we blame ourselves or others or the circumstance, we stay locked into the egoic state. As Carl Jung said, what you resist persists.

One strategy I have used in my life is *gratitude*. While complaint, grumbling, blame, and resistance of any kind to what is will strengthen the ego, an attitude of gratitude will drain the ego of its life substance. Another strategy is selfless *service*. A friend uses the acronym DSFSQ to remind herself that when feeling stress, she should "do something for someone, quick!" But service can be egoic in nature; if you help someone in order to feel good about yourself or to get a compliment or a reward, it does not help you to move beyond egoic entrapment.

Think of the ego this way: the ego is like gravity. Unless you can achieve "escape velocity" by loving it all, the ego will pull you back into its view of reality. Enlightenment is the goal for many spiritual seekers. To reach enlightenment, you must reach escape velocity from the seductive grasp of egoic consciousness.

Another technique I recommend in this book is the conscious use of the Enneagram. The Enneagram, a psycho-spiritual tool, is very useful is spotting, through self-observation, your habitual patterns of thought, emotion and belief. The system illustrates nine basic types of egoic consciousness; everyone, from any culture, is one of these nine types. Once you discover your type and its habitual tendencies of thought, emotion and behavior, you can interrupt your unconscious pattern and choose another response from your awakened consciousness. As you practice self-observation and personal responsibility, you can move into an awakened state where the heart and the mind work together to produce a reality that is not burdened with fear thoughts. The domain of the ego is the domain of fear. Why? Because, at a very deep level, the egoic mind knows that living disconnected from the energy that is moving the cosmos (the afore-mentioned Divine Design) is a very dangerous place to be.

So, as we heal our shadows, express gratitude for all of our experiences, offer selfless service to enhance the well-being of the whole, and practice self-observation through the Enneagram, we can move into what I call the awakened state of consciousness. This doesn't mean that there are no longer any challenges to life; it simply means you now have the tools to deal with whatever comes...with total love and acceptance.

Let me emphasize this last point: loving it all *does not* mean your life will be smooth; quite the contrary. As shadow elements arise to be cleared out, there can be a lot of pain and discomfort. Healing does not always feel good or even "spiritual"; as we come to deal with our shadows, the repressed pain will inevitably come up. How can we find peace in the midst of this storm? Experiencing life's bliss and agony, ecstasy and despair...that is the journey. By staying with all that comes up, and by loving it all, no matter how it feels, you can finish the journey home, right to the eternal present moment.

To Pray Without Ceasing

Whatever arises,
Let me dwell in the secret place of the Most High.
Let there be a place of stillness in the midst of turmoil.
Let there be a place of ease amid disease.
Let there be a place of order in the chaos.
Let there be a place of love and beauty in the midst of fear and ugliness.
Let me presence be a beacon of enfolding radiance in every circumstance.

-Martin Exeter

Author Biography

David K. Banner, PhD was the Professor of Leadership at the Dahl School of Business, Viterbo University, La Crosse, WI until 2008; he has now retired from university teaching. He currently mentors PhD students in Leadership and Organization Change at Walden University in Minneapolis. From 2003-2007, he was the Director of the innovative, values-based MBA program at Viterbo, essentially starting the program from scratch, recruiting students, setting up a Board of Advisors, hiring and mentoring faculty and getting the program accredited. Prior to that, he was the only chaired professor (The Napoleon Hill Professor of Leadership) at the Eckhart School of Business, University of the Pacific, Stockton, CA. All in all, he spent 33years in university teaching in Canada, the US, Australia, and the Netherlands. He is the author of 6 books, 30 journal articles, and 35 conference papers on transformational leadership, self-management, new paradigm organization design, ethics and integrity in business and related topics. In his varied career, he has been an aerospace engineer for NASA, a management consultant for Peat, Marwick, Mitchell (an international accounting/consulting firm), an entrepreneur, a university professor and an author.(www.davidkbanner.com)

He currently resides in Viroqua, WI, a small southwestern Wisconsin town where he was a member of the Vernon County Board of Supervisors, 5 Board sub-committees, The Board of Pleasant Ridge Waldorf school and a member of its Finance Committee, a founding member of the Youth Initiative High School (Waldorf-inspired), and he has served on the Historical Society, the Comprehensive Planning Committee and the Board of the Viroqua Food Coop. David loves life and he samples from its varied aspects freely and with gusto!

27423964R00084

Made in the USA
Charleston, SC
07 March 2014